A Reader's Guide to Modern Irish Drama

A Reader's Guide to Modern Irish Drama

Sanford Sternlicht

Syracuse University Press

Copyright © 1998 by Syracuse University Press
Syracuse, New York 13244-5160
All Rights Reserved

First Edition 1998
99 00 01 02 03   6 5 4 3 2

The paper used in this publication meet the minimum requirements of
American National Standard for Information Sciences—Permanence of
Paper for Printed Library Materials, ANSI Z39.48-1984.●‾

Library of Congress Cataloging-in-Publication Data

Sternlicht, Sanford V.
A reader's guide to modern Irish drama / Sanford Sternlicht.
Includes bibliographical references (p.   ) and index.
ISBN 0-8156-2773-4 (alk. paper). — ISBN 0-8156-0525-0 (pbk. :
alk. paper)
1. English drama—Irish authors—History and criticism—handbooks,
manuals, etc. 2. English drama—20th century—History and
criticism—Handbooks, manuals, etc. 3. English drama—19th century—
History and criticism—Handbooks, manuals, etc. 4. Ireland—In
literature—Handbooks, manuals, etc. I. Title. II. Series.
PR8789.S76   1998
822.009'9417—dc21   98-4927

Manufactured in the United States of America

Contents

Preface

The genesis of this book was in my teaching of Modern Irish Drama at Syracuse University and at Trinity College, Dublin for many summers under the auspices of the Syracuse University Ireland program. In teaching these courses I have found that excellent anthologies of plays are available but there is no up-to-date handbook in print that satisfactorily provides the information necessary to support the course and help students understand both the background of modern Irish drama and the scope of this great ongoing artistic, cultural, and intellectual achievement of which the Irish people and Irish Americans are so justifiably proud.

I feel that students of modern Irish drama, as well as that part of the general reading public in the English-speaking world who have come to enjoy the fine contemporary plays of Brian Friel, Frank McGuinness, Sebastian Barry, and other Irish playwrights at work today, want and need to know some Irish history of this troubled century and earlier times. To begin with, they need to learn the significance of the Irish Literary Revival in the late nineteenth century. Closely linked to this are the story of the Irish National Theatre Society, affectionately known as the Abbey, the greatest national theater in the Western World; the history of Irish drama and theater; and the achievements of the most significant

Irish dramatists of the twentieth century. Lastly, they need to know the composition and nature of the theater world in Ireland today. *A Reader's Guide to Modern Irish Drama* attempts to meet these needs.

Several academics, writers, directors, and actors helped me with this book. I especially wish to thank the following: Christopher Fitz-Simon, a critic, theater historian, director, and actor so very deserving of the esteem and affection his peers have for him; Judy Friel, Acting Literary Manager of the Abbey Theatre, who has been so generous with her time, and so willing to fling much needed information for me across the Atlantic; Dr. Robert Mandel, Director of the Syracuse University Press, who encouraged me from the beginning to do this project; my friend the polymath, Professor James MacKillop, who never failed to answer a question; and my colleagues in the English Department of Syracuse University, who have always made me feel that I was a part of a proud and purposeful intellectual adventure. Additionally, I wish to thank those friends of mine who provided me with information on contemporary dramatists, plays, and performances: Dr. Liam Kennedy of Queen's University, Belfast, and Mrs. Dorothea Nelson of Syracuse, New York.

Syracuse, New York   Sanford Sternlicht
December 1997

Backgrounds

1
...

Early Irish History

Contemporary Irish society is a moving point in a continuum of evolving, superseding, incorporating cultures created by migration, conquest, colonization, imperial domination, religious and racial conflict and prejudice, and an overriding belief in a people's coherence, unity, and destiny. This destiny began with the aboriginal settlers of prehistoric Ireland who crossed the land bridge from what is now Scotland some ten thousand years ago and were followed by Neolithic herders, and then farmers six thousand years ago who cleared vast tracts of arable land out of the ubiquitous forests and built the great passage tombs like Newgrange. In the Bronze Age the Beaker people brought metallurgy to Ireland, followed in the third century B.C. by the most westerly expansion of the Celts and the Iron Age.

Celtic civilization created an heroic epoch, using Irish, the native Celtic language of Ireland (sometimes referred to as Gaelic or Irish Gaelic), to produce the first vernacular literature of Western Europe as well as a glorious high culture. Although waxing and waning over the centuries, this culture remains an inspiration, a foundation, an architectonic, and the pride of contemporary Irish life.

The Imperial Romans in Britain knew about Ireland but chose not to invade the island noted for its fierce warriors and rapacious pirates because they already had enough difficulty with those unconquered Celtic Britons and Picts surrounding the perimeter of Britannia. When Rome's decline accelerated in the fifth century A.D., and the legions protecting Roman Britain were withdrawn, Irish raiders as well as Germanic ones began to plunder the disintegrating colony. A young Romanized Christian Celt named Patricius was captured by Irish slavers and taken across the Irish Sea. After servitude as a shepherd in Ireland, he made his way to the Continent for ordination as a priest and then returned to the land of his former captors as one of Christianity's first missionaries.

In the next century the great Irish monasteries like Armagh, St. Kevin's Glendalough, and St. Columba's Iona in the Hebrides off Scotland were founded. These monasteries flourished and, through the dedication and perseverance of their scribes, preserved Roman and Greek literature. Thus, with the conversion of the pagan Germans, Goths, Franks, and Vandals and the extension of the Irish monastic movement to Britain and the Continent, classical culture was reintroduced to Western Europe, Christianity was revitalized, and an intellectual, philosophical, ecclesiastic bulwark was built that helped the West to withstand the onslaught of Islam from the east and south later in the Middle Ages.

Celtic Ireland after St. Patrick was Christian and princely. Possessed of relative peace and surplus food production, it consequently could support a high culture. Many warrior chiefs gave fealty to the kings of the four traditional provinces: Ulster, Leinster, Munster, and Connaught. Eventually, a titular high king, crowned at Tara, reigned loosely over all. Then the first of the historical invasions began.

The Viking terror commenced in 795 A.D., and a partial Scandinavian occupation remained in effect for over two hundred years, resulting in Ireland's isolation from Continental Christian culture. It also led to the founding of Ireland's first cities: Dublin, Cork, and Limerick, among others. The great High King Brian Boru, who reigned from 1002 to 1014, contained the Vikings and their Irish allies in Leinster and died victorious in battle at Clontarf.

But next came the Normans from Wales in 1169 under Strongbow. He was supported by the English King Henry II, to whom most Irish kings and bishops submitted, and Ireland began eight hundred years of conflict with England, a struggle that in Northern Ireland continues to this day.

Again and again over the centuries, civil wars and rebellions brought English kings and troops to subdue the populace and lay waste the land. The Tudor and Stuart governments began the plantation system in Ulster to pacify the rebellious northern portion of what was in reality the first English colony. They moved Protestant colonists from England and Scotland into the towns and onto the land, displacing the native Irish, most of whom had resisted the Reformation and remained loyal to the Church of Rome.

When both the Catholic South and Loyalist Ulster rebelled against the Puritan Commonwealth government of England, Cromwell arrived in Ireland in 1649, destroying Drogheda and Wexford while massacring much of their populations, and then banishing Catholic nobles and landowners to the remote West.

The Restoration of the British monarchy brought peace to Ireland but also continued repression of Catholics. In 1688 the Glorious Revolution in England deposed the Catholic king James II, and the next year he arrived in Ireland to fight his Protestant successor William III for the English crown. Defeated in 1690 at the Battle of the Boyne, an event celebrated by Northern Irish Protestants to this day, James fled to France. With the final defeat of James's many loyal Catholic supporters at Aughrim in 1691, the fate of the Irish was sealed, and they were to be ruled by a Protestant England and a Protestant Ascendancy for the next 230 years.

The infamous Penal Laws—restrictions on Catholics' religious freedom, participation in public life, and inheritance rights, as well as on the right to vote, to bear arms, to receive higher education, to own land, or to own a horse—were enacted early in the eighteenth century. Catholicism, which became a barely tolerated unofficial religion, was embraced by the vast majority of the Irish people, who in the course of the century slowly undermined many of the provisions of the Penal Laws. The impetus for equality and political freedom for all Irish people began its historical two-pronged assault on colonial rule and privilege: legislation and militant action. Inspired by the French Revolution, Wolfe Tone led the unsuccessful revolt of the United Irishmen in 1798, followed in 1803 by the even less successful Robert Emmet Rising.

To obtain greater control of the country for both London and the Irish Protestant Ascendancy, the Irish Parliament in Dublin was dissolved with the Act of Union in 1800, and Dublin, once the second city of the British empire, began a long decline. The Act was a setback for those Irish people, Catholic and Protestant alike, who dreamed of an Independent Ireland or at least Home Rule. But Catholic Emancipation by peaceful means was underway, led by Daniel O'Connell, "the Liberator." Just before the Wolfe Tone revolt, Roman Catholics obtained the right to vote and other civil rights. Then in 1829, Catholics were permitted to hold seats in the Parliament in London. Later, in 1869, the Church of Ireland (Anglican) was disestablished, and the Irish Protestant bishops lost their seats in the British House of Lords.

The great watershed event in nineteenth-century Irish history, which has had a lasting effect on world history and has scarred the Irish psyche, was the famine of 1845–48, brought about by the combination of the potato blight, successive crop failures of that staple of Irish peasant's diet, and the impotence of the British government in London to implement massive, practical, and timely relief efforts—actions that would have been antithetical to the laissez-faire economic principles of early capitalism.

"The Great Hunger," as it is commonly known, resulted in the loss of nearly one-half of Ireland's pre-famine population of eight million, through starvation, disease, and emigration. The present-day existence of large Irish communities in the United States, Canada, Australia, New Zealand, and elsewhere is largely due to that terrible event. And another legacy is the widely held belief by many Irish people that the government in London did little to relieve starvation because of racist attitudes towards the poor, Catholic, Irish-speaking peasants of western Ireland, a population the government seemed to be content to be rid, of one way or another.

Another armed rising failed in that year of failed revolutions, 1848, and the nationalists of the Young Ireland movement faded away. A decade later, the Irish Republican Brotherhood and the Fenian Brotherhood were formed to take up the cause of Irish freedom from Great Britain. The Fenians failed in their rising of 1867. Then the legislative tack was tried again and home rule, tenants' rights, and land reform became the political road to equality and the hope of eventual full emancipation. Charles Stewart Parnell, who became head of the Irish Parliamentary Party in 1881, brought Ireland close to Home Rule in the Gladstone governments but, tragically, was disgraced and dismissed because of a divorce scandal. When the nineteenth century ended, most Irish Catholics were determined to achieve some degree of independence from Britain, and most of the Irish Protestants of the North, still loyal to the Crown, were equally determined to remain in the United Kingdom of Great Britain and Ireland.

2
•••

The Century of Destiny

Positions hardened dramatically with the coming of the twentieth century. Sinn Fein was established under Arthur Griffith in 1908, and three illegal armies were formed in 1913: the Ulster Volunteer Force in the North; and, in the South, the Irish Citizen Army and the Irish Volunteers. The island was racked with labor strikes as, disastrously, in 1914 Home Rule for Ireland was put off until the cessation of World War I, when it was to be implemented after the peace treaty, with a Northern Irish Parliament and another for the rest of the country. But it was too late for the Nationalists. In the fateful year of 1916, men from the Irish Revolutionary Brotherhood and the Irish Citizen Army, led by the poet Patrick Pearse and the labor union leader James Connolly, proclaimed the Irish Republic in Dublin on 24 April and fought the British Army for five days. The subsequent drawn-out execution of fifteen Republican prisoners from the Easter Rising by the British shocked much of the world and galvanized the Irish majority into support of full independence from Britain even as thousands of Irishmen from Ulster and from the South were dying for Britain in the trenches of France and Belgium.

In December 1918 Republicans were victorious in general elections. They convened their own Irish parliament, the Dail Eireann, in Dublin in January 1919, while the American born Eamon de Valera, sole surviving commander in the Easter Rising and later prime minister and then president of Ireland, toured America, attempting to obtain support for Irish claims at the Versailles Peace Conference. Simultaneously, the Anglo-Irish War, the Irish War of Independence, broke out, with the result that martial law was instituted by the occupation forces; and ambushes, atrocities, and burnings marked a savage guerrilla war between Republicans, under the brilliant tactician Michael Collins, and the Constabulary and the notorious Black and Tans, a paramilitary force of British ex-soldiers attempting on orders from London to terrorize the Irish into submission. Then Collins and his motorized flying squads and urban guerrillas were victorious, and the war-weary British finally requested a peace conference in 1921.

The Anglo-Irish Treaty providing for the partition of Ireland into the Free State (so called because the British government could not stomach the term Republic of Ireland) in the South, and Ulster remaining as a part of the United Kingdom was approved by the Dail in 1922. The tragic Irish Civil War ensued as anti-Treaty Republicans, with de Valera as the political leader, fought the new government army and were defeated; General Michael Collins was killed in the conflict. The new state thus was tragically born in the blood of those who had fought together against the British but were now killing each other. Although hostilities finally ceased in 1923, the illegal underground Irish Republican Army continues to this day to attempt to negate the terms of the Treaty and force Britain out of Northern Ireland.

Deciding to take the legislative route once more, de Valera left Sinn Fein in 1926 to found a new political party, Fianna Fail, and became head of government in 1932, first banning and eventually proscribing the IRA by 1936. Under a new constitution, the Irish Free State became Eire in 1937. As World War II broke out, Eire declared neutrality, and de Valera skillfully managed to keep the country out of the war despite Anglo-American pressure and the German bombing of Dublin. But because of de Valera's outdated economic and social policies, Ireland did not participate fully in the postwar European recovery.

In 1949 the Irish Republic was declared with the hope and intention of bringing internal peace to the island, but in the 1950s and 1960s the IRA continued its sporadic harassment of Britain and Northern Ireland, while the Ulster government allowed economic discrimination and occasional intimidation of its Catholic minority. In 1955, Ireland joined the United Nations, and in 1961 it tried but failed to be admitted to the European Economic Community. Ireland was finally added to the European Union in 1973.

Set up in 1967 to fight discrimination, the Northern Irish Civil Rights Association signaled a new militancy for the Catholic minority in Ulster, and the "Troubles" began the next year, lasting until the truce of 1994, which stood only eighteen months. As of 1997 a new IRA cease-fire has precipitated all-party negotiations that may lead to a peaceful settlement. The years since 1968 have seen assassinations of British officials and soldiers, IRA bombing campaigns in Britain, hunger strikes by IRA members in prison, and loyalist opposition to possible Anglo-Irish agreements. Two of the worst events occurred in 1972: "Bloody Sunday," when British soldiers shot to death fourteen Nationalist marchers; and "Bloody Friday," when an IRA bomb killed eleven people in Belfast,

But Eire moves on. The "special position" of the Roman Catholic Church has been eliminated from the constitution. A referendum has permitted the introduction of divorce into Irish society for the first time since 1925. Mary Robinson became the first female president of Ireland in 1991. Membership in the European Union has helped Ireland economically, and the country is more prosperous than it has ever been in its history. As of this writing, December 1997, peace talks continue, and there is hope that the long conflict between the Nationalists and Loyalists in the North may be resolved peacefully, with the goodwill of the vast majority of the Irish people and perhaps the help of other countries, such as the United States. With an outstanding educational system, some of the most fertile land in Europe, close connections with America as well as the rest of Europe, burgeoning high-tech industries, and the youngest population in Europe, Ireland is moving into the twenty-first century with high hopes and great expectations.

3

The Literary Tradition

The Celtic Revival and the Celtic Twilight

With Catholic emancipation in the nineteenth century the Irish people began to look back on their medieval cultural inheritance, the literature and the art of the early Christian era, and to reconstruct the past in fine and applied art. Most significantly, a renewed pride in the ancient tongue revived the use and study of the Irish language and probably saved it from extinction. In music the sentimental and patriotic lyrics and scores of Thomas Moore contributed to the Celtic Revival as did the poetry of James Clarence Mangan and the poetry and translations of Samuel Ferguson. The Gaelic League, founded in 1893, promulgated the teaching of the Irish language; by inaugurating Irish festivals of singing, dancing, piping, fiddling, and poetry recitals, the League counteracted the feelings of inferiority of many native Irish speakers, who had been indoctrinated into believing that English was the superior tongue and that English culture was more sublime, advanced, and of greater value than Irish culture.

"The Celtic Twilight" as a term is a coinage of William Butler Yeats, Ireland's greatest poet and arguably the foremost poet of the English language in the twentieth century. This term, which he employed as the title of his book of Irish folklore published in

1893, is used to describe the literary and artistic mood in Ireland in the last decade of the nineteenth century and the first of the twentieth, a romantic mood of shadowy mysticism and mournfulness. Its misty view of ancient Ireland—an Irish version of Pre-Raphaelitism—may have been inspired by Matthew Arnold's 1867 Oxford lecture "On the Study of Celtic Literature." Although the realists and modernists who soon followed reacted against the flowery, self-referential, pastoral, heavily imagistic early poetry of Yeats and that of his followers and denigrated it, the international public loved the verse and the pseudo-archaic tales for the beauty of their language and the power of their sentiments.

The Irish Literary Renaissance

Also referred to as the Irish Literary Revival, the Irish Literary Renaissance, a phenomenon coterminous with the Celtic Twilight, grew out of the historical writings of Standish O'Grady that celebrated the Heroic Age of Ireland for a people thirsty for heroes and heroines. It also was influenced greatly by the nationalist fervor instilled in young writers by that old Fenian, John O'Leary, who was released from an English prison in 1884 and returned to Ireland to help educate the younger generation and build an Irish consciousness.

Yeats founded the Irish Literary Society of London in 1891 and the National Literary Society in Dublin the next year. He was indeed a great *founder* (his first founding was the Dublin Hermetic Society in 1885), later helping to found the Irish Literary Theatre in 1897, the Irish National Theatre Society in 1902, and the venerable Abbey Theatre in 1904. Indeed, Yeats was the true father of the Irish Literary Renaissance.

Although the writers of the Irish Literary Renaissance worked almost exclusively in the English language, their English was in various ways influenced, inflected, and subverted by underlying Irish linguistic patterns and lexicon. Theirs was a remarkable outpouring of world-class literature from a small nation with a tiny population, afloat on the western edge of Europe. This period of high creativity has been given widely differing dates; in a way, the Renaissance continues, for little Ireland is very big indeed when it comes to internationally recognized writers (two of them have recently won the Nobel Prize for Literature, Samuel Beckett in 1969 and Seamus Heaney in 1996). I offer these dates as workable and useful: 1885 to the death of Yeats in 1939, for in the sense of dominating influence, Yeats *was* the Irish Literary Renaissance.

The writers of the period are a pantheon of literary achievement in poetry, fiction, and drama. Besides Yeats they include James Joyce, of course, and Lady Gregory, Edith Sommerville and Violet Martin (Sommerville and Ross), John Millington Synge, George Moore, Katherine Tynan, George Fitzmaurice, Sean O'-Casey, AE (George William Russell), Padraic Colum, Thomas MacDonagh, Joseph Campbell, James Stephens, Austin Clarke, Frank O'Connor, Peadar O'Donnell, Sean O'Faolain, Liam O'Flaherty, Lord Dunsany, Seamus O'Kelly, George Shiels, Lennox Robinson, Brinsley MacNamara, Elizabeth Bowen, and the young Samuel Beckett, among others.

In the period of the Irish Literary Renaissance, Irish writing moved from nineteenth-century romanticism into early twentieth-century modernism, making a magnificent contribution to what became the dominant literary high style of the century of world war, revolution, genocide, population explosion, and technological advance beyond the wildest dreams of past humanity.

A Silver Age

Irish writers have continued to show remarkable creativity and hold a significant position in the wide world of belletristic writing during the second half of the twentieth century. It is not just Nobel laureates who are recognized internationally, but also many other excellent writers. The dramatist Brian Friel commands a world stage. Poets, playwrights, and fiction writers of great note include Mary Lavin, Iris Murdoch, Joyce Carey, Louis MacNeice, Michael J. Molloy, Denis Johnston, Michael McLaverty, Benedict Kiley, Brendan Behan, Patrick Kavanagh, Thomas Kinsella, John B. Keene, Eugene McCabe, Thomas Kilroy, Tom Murphy, Tom Mac Intyre, Michael Longley, John McGahern, John Montague, Brendan Kinnelly, Derek Mahon, William Trevor, Brian Moore, Jennifer Johnston, Edna O'Brien, Derek Mahon, Julia O'Faolain, Eavan Boland, John McGahern, Bernard McLaverty, Paul Durcan, Eiléan Ní Chuilleanáin, Michael Ó Siadhail, Hugh Maxton, Medbh McGuckian, Nuala Ní Dhomhnaill, Paul Muldoon, Frank McGuinness, Stewart Parker, John Banville, Roddy Doyle, Maeve Binchy, James Plunkett, Christy Brown, Paul Muldoon, Brendan Kennelly, Richard Murphy, Seamus Deane, Pat McCabe, Colm Taibin, and, of course, Seamus Heaney.

4
...

The Irish Theater

Theater came to Ireland in the Middle Ages with the Anglo-Norman invaders. Mystery plays, which were based on the Bible, and morality plays, which served as dramatized allegorical sermons, were performed in the towns, under the auspices of the Church and guilds, on holidays like Whitsuntide and Corpus Christi. Because Ireland remained mostly Catholic even after Henry VIII brought the Reformation to England and those areas of Ireland under English control, the religious drama continued unabated until Oliver Cromwell's assault on Irish civilization.

Previously, Ireland's first professional theater, the Werburgh Street Theatre, was opened in Dublin, near Dublin Castle, in 1637 but lasted only four years. There the first play on a purely Irish subject, *St. Patrick for Ireland*, written by the resident dramatist James Shirley, was performed in 1639.

In 1692, after the Restoration of Charles II to the English throne, Dublin's Theatre Royal, Smock Alley, opened, and once again Irish playwrights had a local venue. But like the Werburgh Theatre, Smock Alley, located in what is now the Temple Bar district of Dublin, was a provincial stage, where the fare was primarily imports from London.

In the late seventeenth century and in the eighteenth century, Irish writers most frequently moved to London to try to make

16

their fortunes. One of the most notable was William Congreve, who left Dublin for London in 1689 at the age of nineteen; and his four great comedies, *The Old Bachelor, The Double Dealer, Love for Love,* and *The Way of the World* were all first performed there. Derry-born George Farquhar began his theatrical career as a Smock Alley actor and then moved to London, where his plays *Love and a Bottle, The Constant Couple, Sir Harry Wildhair, The Recruiting Officer,* and his masterpiece, *The Beaux' Stratagem,* were produced with varying success.

Many other Irish playwrights followed Congreve and Farquhar across the Irish Sea, while the great actors of the English stage came over to perform in Dublin, including David Garrick. In the mid-eighteenth century the multitalented Oliver Goldsmith, who had left Ireland to seek literary fame in London, achieved theater immortality by writing what is arguably the greatest English-language comedy of the enlightened century, *She Stoops to Conquer.*

The Derry-born actor Charles Macklin starred in famous productions of Shakespeare and other plays on the London stage, becoming in addition the first Irish-born actor-manager. The second, remaining in Dublin to manage Smock Alley, was Thomas Sheridan, who earned the undying affection of actors by banning the practice of allowing members of the audience to sit on the stage and by actually paying actors contracted salaries! His son, the sharp-witted Richard Brinsley Sheridan, wrote two masterpieces for the late eighteenth-century London stage, *The Rivals,* and *The School for Scandal.* The famous London actor-manager William Macready was also an Irishman.

Clearly, the late seventeenth and eighteenth century established that the Irish genius is for comedy. It appears as true today as then.

In the nineteenth century the great Irish actors were Barry Sullivan and Tyrone Power, ancestor of the American film star of the 1930–1950 period. The first Tyrone Power perfected the stage-

Irish character, a comic caricature that now seems as painful and out-of-place as a racial joke. The most commercially successful Irish dramatist of the nineteenth century was the prolific and internationally famous writer of melodramas, Dion Boucicault, most admired in Ireland for his sentimental trilogy *Colleen Bawn, Arrah-na-Pogue,* and *The Shaughraun.*

From the eighteenth century through the nineteenth, theaters in Europe grew larger and thus less intimate, partly to accommodate larger audiences (and earn more money for the managers) and partly because of the emphasis on spectacular melodramas, opera, Shakespearean productions, and various multiscene extravaganzas. The first new theaters in Dublin were on Aungier, Capel, Fishamble, and Crowe Streets. Nineteenth-century theaters surviving in Dublin are the Gaiety and the Olympia. Belfast's Grand Opera House, severely damaged in an IRA attack, has been restored to its former glory. Almost all of the early theaters in smaller Irish towns have either been abandoned or torn down.

Beyond question, Ireland's great nineteenth-century contribution to world drama was the work of the incomparable Oscar Wilde, perhaps the wittiest person who ever put pen to paper. Born in Dublin, Wilde went to Oxford after Trinity College, Dublin. Later, in London, as a leader of the Aesthetic Movement, Wilde became a controversial but much appreciated public figure who enjoyed outraging conservative society with his wit and his seemingly decadent, *Yellow Book* life-style. His superb plays still grace the boards of theaters everywhere. They include *Lady Windermere's Fan, A Woman of No Importance, An Ideal Husband,* and the greatest English-language comedy—indeed, play—of the nineteenth century, *The Importance of Being Earnest.* As is well known, Wilde's career ended in sexual scandal and his life, alas, in bitter exile.

Born in almost the same year and same city as Oscar Wilde was the long-lived, laughter-loving propagandist and social theorist of a playwright, George Bernard Shaw, the first Irishman to win the Nobel Prize for Literature. Shaw delighted audiences everywhere in the English-speaking world with his thesis comedies that explored problems of gender, poverty, religion, war, and class as Ibsen did in the genre of tragedy. Shaw's legacy to world drama has proved worthy of a festival devoted to his work, and his major plays like *Arms and the Man, The Devil's Disciple, Candida, Man and Superman, The Doctor's Dilemma, Pygmalion,* and *Saint Joan* are continually performed.

Also of great significance is Shaw's one "Irish" play, *John Bull's Other Island,* written for Yeats and the early Abbey in 1904 but then initially declined by Yeats (who, it must be said, never had much sympathy for Shavian thesis comedy), and thus first produced in London instead of Dublin. The play may have been too hot a political potato for the fledgling theater to handle, or it may be that the large cast, multiscene play may have seemed beyond the capabilities of the company and the tiny theater at so early a date. The Abbey finally put on *John Bull's Other Island* in 1914, and it became a perennial favorite in Dublin for many years, never ceasing to provoke heated discourse. The play is a favorite of mine because, besides being wickedly witty, its satire on English-Irish relations seems perennially current. *John Bull's Other Ireland* will be discussed fully later on.

But back to the beginning of a great national theater enterprise. Modern Irish drama and theater began with the founding of the Irish Literary Theatre in 1897 by Yeats, Edward Martyn, and Lady Isabella Augusta Gregory—all playwrights. Yeats wrote poetic drama out of his background in Irish mythology and in accordance with the principles and practices of the French Symbolists. Lady Gregory employed her knowledge of and affection for the Irish peasants who lived around her home in Gort, near Galway, and she found her dramatic models in French comedy. Martyn was a disciple of Henrik Ibsen and a writer of problem plays and social drama.

The Irish Literary Theatre began producing in 1899 with performances of Yeats's symbolic, medieval, poetic drama *The Countess Cathleen* and Martyn's problem play on landlord-tenant relations, *The Heather Field*. The venue was the Antient Concert Hall Rooms, a concert hall seating 800. Other productions were in the grand Victorian theater, the Gaiety. In 1902 the organization, now called the National Dramatic Society, performed Yeats's fiercely nationalistic *Cathleen ni Houlihan* and AE's dreamy *Deidre* in the 300-seat St. Theresa's Hall.

In 1903 the organization became the Irish National Theatre Society, and its theater, familiarly known as the Abbey because of its location, on Lower Abbey Street, opened in 1904 with a performance of Yeats's mythological *On Baile's Strand* and Lady Gregory's peasant comedy *Spreading the News*. The Irish National Theatre Society at the Abbey went on to become and remain one of Europe's most important national repertory theaters, like the Moscow Art Theater, and the earliest modern repertory theater in Europe. The Abbey is a cultural jewel that is not only a source of great pride for the Irish people but also the envy of many nations.

The Abbey's main mission remains primarily but not exclusively to produce plays by Irish playwrights on Irish themes. It has always been to a very large extent a writers' theater. With its inception, ordinary people—peasant farmers, city workers, fisherfolk, back-country people, itinerants, small merchants, the poor, the sick, and the blind—would find a place and a voice on the Irish stage. The foolish and embarrassing, shifty, hot-tempered, lazy, conniving, often drunken, comic "Stage Irishman," speaking in a ludicrously exaggerated accent, was banished except for historical revivals of early works.

Shortly after the Abbey's founding and initial successes, rival companies in Dublin were set up. Most notable was the Irish Theatre Company, 1914–1920, under Edward Martyn, who had broken with his fellow directors of the Abbey. None of the early rivals survived, however.

In the beginning, plays in the Irish language were attempted by the Irish National Theatre Society (such as the folk comedies of Douglas Hyde, later the first president of Ireland under the Constitution of 1937), but with limited success, and most of Ireland's dramatic contributions have been in English. Much later, Taibhdhearc na Gaillimhe, the Irish language theater located in Galway, continued the tradition of performances in Irish but had greater success with translations from other languages. Gael-Linn in Dublin in the 1950s also produced Irish language plays to encourage use of Irish Gaelic. Its greatest success was in 1958 with Brendan Behan's *An Giall* (The Hostage).

Yeats's inspiration and Lady Gregory's managerial skills and diplomacy sustained the Abbey in its infancy and early adolescence. Of course, the timely infusion of money the from English heiress Annie Horniman, a friend of Yeats, proved decisive in the beginning. Yeats and Gregory brought John Millington Synge to the Abbey. The superb one-acters *In the Shadow of the Glen* and *Riders to the Sea* and the full-length masterpieces *The Playboy of the Western World* and *The Well of the Saints* established Synge as the Abbey's leading dramatist in its early years. Yeats and Gregory also discovered the youthful Padraic Colum, whose three plays written in the first decade of the twentieth century, *The Fiddler's House*, *The Land*, and *Thomas Muskerry*, helped bring the peasant play into prominence and obtained a popular audience for the Abbey Theatre and the new Irish drama in general. The country plays of William Boyle and George Fitzmaurice also added to the growth of this audience.

The Abbey needed good actors, and it grew its own, starting with the former amateurs Frank and William Fay, who as performers and directors turned the company and the theater into a professional organization. Others who graced the early twentieth-century Irish stage included Florence Farr, Barry Fitzgerald, Sarah Allgood, Molly Allgood, F. J. McCormack, Moira O'Neill, and Fred O'Donovan. The first two mentioned became world-famous through American film. Later Jack McGowran, Patrick Magee, Cyril Cussack, Milo O'Shea, Siobhán McKenna, and the Shakespearean specialist, Anew McMaster added luster to the Irish stage and in some cases to international cinema.

Ireland's great playwright in the years between the World Wars was Dublin-born Sean O'Casey, who was brought into the theater by Lady Gregory. His reputation rests on the magnificent tragicomic historical trilogy of the birth trauma of the Irish Free State: *The Shadow of a Gunman, Juno and the Paycock,* and *The Plough and the Stars.* Other popular Irish playwrights of the period include George Shiels, St. John Ervine, Teresa Deevey, and Lennox Robinson, who was associated with the Abbey for fifty years as a playwright, manager, and director. In the 1920s the actor, designer, playwright Micheál MacLiammóir and the actor-director Hilton Edwards founded the privately funded Dublin Gate Theatre, which has proved to be one of the century's longest-surviving theater enterprises. The Gate has achieved world renown through the quality of its productions, which emphasize international classics by such modern dramatists as Henrik Ibsen, the founder of modern drama, Eugene O'Neill, and Jean Cocteau, as well as works by Irish playwrights. Although some would deny its existence, the friendly rivalry between the Abbey and Gate over the decades has been to the great advantage of Irish culture.

The old Abbey Theatre consisted of a converted concert hall that had belonged to the Mechanics' Institute; for its lobby or foyer and business offices it had an old bank building that in a yet earlier life had been the Dublin morgue. In 1951 the Abbey burned, and the ruins were torn down. It had been loved by the public and hated by the company. Because the old Abbey's proscenium was only twenty-one feet wide and fifteen feet deep, there was little room for backdrops or shutters and practically no space to build. Consequently, most plays produced there required only a single set, often a room in a farmer's cottage in the West Country.

For fifteen years the company performed in the old Queen's Theatre near Trinity College (now demolished and lamented), where productions were often lacking in distinction, to a large extent because of a paucity of government financial support. But other companies in Dublin and other Irish cities took up the challenge of performing exciting new work. Brendan Behan's play *The Quare Fellow* was turned down by the Abbey company but was produced at the Pike Theatre Club in 1954 founded by one of Ireland's finest directors, Alan Simpson, among others. The Pike also presented the first Irish production of Beckett's *Waiting for Godot* in 1955. At last the new Abbey Theatre opened in 1966, on its original site, in a relatively modest but quite functional building designed by Michael Scott. Today plans are being laid to remodel the thirty-one-year old theater.

Northern Ireland developed its own theater traditions, especially in Belfast. Beginning in 1902, the Ulster Literary Theatre, led by Bulmer Hobson, also encouraged Irish dramatists, deriving its inspiration from the Irish Literary Theatre in the South. After thirty years it was succeeded by the Ulster Group Theatre, which had a twenty-year run. Currently, the Lyric Theatre with its repertory company is the leading venue for drama in Belfast, although it seems that its fare generally is more British and international than Irish. But Belfast, like Dublin, is a theater town. Several smaller companies are continually mounting exciting Irish plays and international hits; Charabanc and Dubbeljoint are outstanding examples. Belfast productions often are seen in Dublin and sometimes tour North America.

Derry's ground-breaking Field Day Company, now seemingly fading out of existence, is forever enshrined in Irish theater history for introducing Brian Friel's *Translations* to an admiring world in 1980, its premier season. Playing all of Ireland and Wales, Scotland, and England too, the new Irish Theatre Company, 1974–1982, brought Irish plays and world classics to provincial cities as well as the capitals. This company included several of Ireland's most talented modern directors, including Joe Dowling and Christopher Fitz-Simon.

From a largely Protestant upper–middle-class outer suburb of Dublin and Trinity College emerged Samuel Beckett, arguably the greatest dramatist of the twentieth century. After Trinity he moved to France, eventually settling there, surviving anti-German Underground action in World War II as a member of the French Resistance, and writing in French and translating his work into English. His existential masterpieces of the 1950s and early 1960s, *Waiting for Godot, Endgame,* and *Happy Days,* profoundly affected and perhaps changed not only the theater of Western culture but the way human beings living in this culture perceive reality and contemplate their own lives. Performed in English, Beckett's plays, if done well, sound Irish and remind culturally aware audiences of Yeats and Synge.

Not as profound as Beckett but certainly making better newspaper copy was the irrepressible, beloved, heavy-drinking and ultimately tragic Dublin-born IRA fighter Brendan Behan, whose reputation was established with the Pike Theatre's production of *The Quare Fellow* in 1954. On that play and *The Hostage* his reputation as a playwright rests. It is interesting to note that Beckett and Behan were writing their major plays at about the same time. How different and yet how similar their values are! Behan is political (an Irish Republican), and Beckett is not so directly. But, of course, Beckett as a Marxist ideologue tempered by existential compassion and ennui is the ultimate political. Both of these Irish playwrights have a weltanschauung that is basically serio-comic—that life is a funny tragedy. In that, their Irishness unites them.

In the forefront of today's host of fine Irish dramatists stand Brian Friel and Frank McGuinness. Friel's reputation was established with *Philadelphia, Here I Come!* (directed by Hilton Edwards) and solidified with world-wide performances of *Translations.* McGuinness's *Observe the Sons of Ulster Marching Towards the Somme* electrified audiences all over Ireland and Britain; his hostage drama *Someone to Watch Over Me* was especially moving for American audiences.

Today the Irish theater appears very much alive and well. In Dublin the Abbey, perennially plagued by financial problems, nevertheless thrives on artistic successes in the production of Irish classics and selected modern and contemporary plays. The Abbey's smaller stage, the Peacock, showcases the performance of a seemingly unending stream of brilliant plays by lesser-known dramatists and younger playwrights, who are often at the beginning of very promising careers.

The Dublin Gate Theatre has added to its international reputation with enthusiastically received tours. The Gaiety delights a popular audience of Irish people and visitors. The Projects Arts Centre provides a compatible venue for the more experimental new plays. A half-dozen or more professional and semiprofessional groups present Irish plays new and old, Shakespeare, Elizabethan and Jacobean drama, European and American plays, and experimental performance theater. The annual Dublin Theatre Festival provides a platform for new work. Dinner theaters are growing in number, and theater in the universities throughout Ireland is flourishing, now providing trained artists for the Irish stage, TV, and cinema.

In Belfast, as noted earlier, the Lyric and several relatively small companies provide exciting and excellent theater. Founded in 1975 in Galway by Garry Hynes, Mick Lally, and Marie Mullen, the Druid Theatre, through spirited productions of new Irish plays and Irish classics, has built a stellar reputation that has extended beyond Ireland's shores. Other cities have very successful repertory and producing companies too, as well as well-equipped, comfortable theaters. And the Irish community theater movement is enviable in its scope, enthusiasm, and quality.

In addition, both Radio Telefis Eireann and the BBC, mighty cultural forces, have encouraged Irish theater artists of all types and significantly helped to sustain and grow the audience for the Irish theater.

The world of scholarship has also embraced and supported Irish drama and theater. A steady flow of books and articles on Irish culture cascades from international presses and periodicals. Useful and informative Usenet newsgroups and sites on the World Wide Web abound on the Internet. The American Conference of Irish Studies and the International Association for the Study of Anglo-Irish Literature, along with Irish Studies programs in American, British, and Canadian universities, sustain interest in Irish drama and theater, as well as providing a continuing international audience for modern and postmodern Irish plays and building support for works yet to come.

At the very beginning of the twentieth century, a handful of patriotic would-be playwrights and actors in a small country working in a makeshift theater, to their own astonishment, created one of history's great national repertory theaters and a dramatic tradition that is a wonder of modern culture. Today Irish theater can anticipate a bright future.

Playwrights and Plays

5
•••

A Thematic Introduction

Not surprisingly, many themes weave their ways in and out of the one-hundred-year history of modern Irish drama. Most pervading is the theme of nationalism, first emphatically introduced by Yeats and in the 1920s turned into a subject of satire and derision by O'Casey (for which he was not forgiven by some). Modern Irish drama evolved from the nationalistic movement at the turn of the twentieth century. It was conceived out of the energy and the ardor of those Irish writers who believed that the Irish nation was awaiting a rebirth as a self-governing people. Yeats called upon the ancient heroic past to provide thematic subjects for the new Irish drama, and Colum found heroism in peasant life and action in the recent past, such as in the Land War of the 1880s. One can reasonably argue that modern Irish nationalism came into being partly because of the fervor of the Anglo-Irish writers of the late nineteenth and early twentieth centuries and that it was under the leadership of poets that the Rising of 1916 occurred.

The great and ancient theme of Anglo-Irish conflict is somewhat muted in the present, pushed to the background by the related and derived theme of Unionist-Republican conflict and the fight for civil rights in Ulster. The Anglo-Irish struggle is primarily a cultural one now, with the smaller nation physically cut off from the rest of Europe by its far larger and wealthier neighboring first cousin, with whom somehow there must be a rapprochement. Related to this theme is the theme of intermarriage between Catholics and Protestants, often expressed in tragic Romeo and Juliet scenarios.

But the peasant drama too had themes that did not play, so to speak, on the national political stage. These themes, close to the hearts and ever in the minds of ordinary people, included the painful problems of exile and emigration as they impacted family, community, and even nation; of leaving and sometimes returning; and of the devastating breaking of traditionally strong family ties. Although Ireland's chief export is no longer human talent, the last theme is still current in the nation and in the wider Irish world, as witnessed, for example, by the continuing success of revivals of Friel's *Philadelphia, Here I Come.*

Then there are the marriage wars and the struggle of the young to overcome the impediments of arranged marriages when they desire to pursue their own destinies. There is also the struggle for land ownership and inheritance in a country where for centuries it was nearly impossible for a Roman Catholic peasant to own land. When land ownership was finally possible, the parcels acquired could not sustain the traditionally large families; second and third sons had to leave the farm and make their way in the wide world as best they could, and daughters were married off to whatever men could support them.

The theme of poverty, of course, persisted as long as the actuality. Another prominent theme is the breaking away from the power of the father by the young, who seek through education and enterprise a life off the land and out of the clutches of the patriarchal family and the collaborating Church. The past themes are, of course, eminently exportable because American, British, and Commonwealth audiences, with their large percentage of citizens of Irish or partially Irish ancestry, are nostalgically curious about life, especially rural life, in the world of their great-grandparents.

Today in Ireland the archromantic, mythic, heroic theme is much out of fashion, and peasant life seems remote. To a nation that is primarily city dwelling, forward looking, and trying to dilute the legacy of a seemingly backward past, the ways of the old peasant now appear to be no longer pertinent or even quaint—useful largely as the subject of satire or farce and as contrast.

Related to the dramatic, historically and theatrically speaking, is the now fading theme of the disruption of rural life resulting from the migration to the cities in the post–World War II era. This theme is generally presented from the perspective of the new, young city dweller, who is simultaneously fascinated, happy, lonely, impressionable, rootless, and lost in his or her new environment.

The stagnation of provincial life, caused by the inertia resulting from the crushing alliance of Church, temporal power, and local hierarchy dedicated to maintaining the status quo in society, is a theme that has continued in Irish drama with little abatement since the beginning of the twentieth century. It is a consequence not only of colonialism but also of the economically conservative De Valera era. This stagnation, or the sense that it still persists, has caused the incorrect perception by many young people that Irish culture is inadequate and inferior to that of other Western nations, thus feeding a desire for imported values and culture, particularly from America and Britain. It is as if Ireland stood as a poor neighbor between two wealthy ones who don't see her or regard her and are content to talk over her head. Postmodern Irish dramatists have made much of this perception.

A lighter perennial theme in Irish drama is the love of the Irish of taking flights of fancy, letting imagination have its head, reveling in fantasy and what might have been and yet might be—and telling it with gusto, of course.

On the very dark side there is the theme of slanderous misogyny: women are predatory, prurient, and ever disrespectful or despising of their husbands, their lovers, and sometimes even their fathers. Counterbalancing this theme is that of the brutal, sometimes drunken father, politically and materially powerless but the terror of the home. The current manifestation of this ever-present theme can be seen in the work of women writers, who comprehend and express Irish women's dissatisfaction with their role in society, articulating that dissatisfaction in their eschewing of violent history, recognizing the weakening of the traditional moral alliance between mother and priest against the father's economic and legal power, and evidencing disappointment in Irish men as faithful companions and adequate sexual partners.

Like most societies, Ireland's is engaged in the business of reenvisioning and reimaging its history. Depicting those activities is continually a function of drama. Because theater is such a popular medium in Ireland, history revisited—particularly recent history—remains a major preoccupation of contemporary dramatists.

In the broadest terms Irish drama in the twentieth century has followed two paths: the path of realism or naturalism and the path of expressionism. Despite the romanticism, lyricism, and mysticism of Yeats, the Abbey Theatre has primarily followed the realistic path pioneered early in the century by Lady Gregory, Martyn, and Colum and continued with such early 1920s masterpieces as O'Casey's Anglo-Irish and Civil War trilogy—but not his expressionistic *The Silver Tassie (1929)*, which, like Denis Johnston's surrealistic *The Old Lady Says No!* (1929), was rejected by the Abbey. Significantly, Johnston changed the original title of his play, *Shadowdance*, to *The Old Lady Says No!* because someone wrote those words on his returned manuscript ("the old lady" was Lady Gregory, of course). Expressionist, surrealistic, darkly satirical and sardonic plays found their venue for much of the century at the Gate, the Peacock, and the Pike theaters as well as at little theaters of the Off-Broadway type in Dublin, Belfast, and elsewhere.

These perennial Irish themes have served tragedy, comedy, melodrama, and farce. The Irish adore comedy, yet it is no wonder that Beckett, in *Endgame*, has Nell say, "Nothing is funnier than unhappiness."

6

Lady Gregory
(1852–1932)

Born Isabella Augusta Persse, twelfth in a family of sixteen children, at Roxborough, County Galway, in the West of Ireland, and educated privately, Lady Gregory was a child of the Protestant Anglo-Irish Ascendancy, whose manorial estates in rural Ireland, and the accompanying town houses, were sites of political unionism, authority, and gentility. But in childhood and adolescence Augusta, as she was always called by family and friends, developed artistic sensibilities, and she grew sympathetic to the republican views of many of the common people of the estates and the small towns and villages. Sean O'Casey, born in the Dublin slums, was quite correct when late in Lady Gregory's life he wrote to her: "You can always walk with your head up. . . . remember you had to fight against your birth into position and comfort, as others had to fight against their birth into hardship and poverty."

Lady Gregory read Finian political tracts, and she collected folk ballads. As a young woman she tried to help local farmers in their economic struggle with wholesalers and retailers of their produce. As a married woman she wrote pamphlets supporting certain liberal Irish causes that were intended to ease British control, but she was against Home Rule for Ireland.

In 1852, Augusta Persse married Sir William Gregory and

came to live at Coole Park, near Gort, County Galway. The mansion, surrounding park, and supporting farms became a place of inspiration and sustenance for many Irish writers because of Lady Gregory's generous patronage. Yeats came almost every summer to enjoy the park and the lake, the good food and conversation, and the opportunity to relax, think, and create. No wonder that when he chose a home for his bride and family to come he settled only a few miles away from Coole.

At the time of their marriage, Sir William was a widower of sixty-three and Lady Gregory was twenty-eight. She had suitors near her own age, but her mother had rejected them as not having enough social status for the family. The Gregorys had one child, Robert, much beloved by his mother, but he was killed in action with the Royal Flying Corps in 1918. One of Yeats's most famous poems, "An Irish Airman Foresees His Death," was written to try to help comfort his grieving friend.

When Lady Gregory's husband died in 1892, she commenced to edit his autobiography for publication, and she wore black for the rest of her life. Most importantly, however, she served her apprenticeship as a writer in this dutiful work, developing a clear and fluid style. Also significant was her ability to make and keep friends whether or not they agreed with her political views. Lady Gregory studied Irish Gaelic with her son and became fluent in the language.

Finally, she began what became a major architectonic of her life as a writer: the collection and editing of West Country folklore and history, sometimes in the local Kiltartan Irish English dialect. Her published works in this genre include *Poets and Dreamers* (1903), *A Book of Saints and Wonders* (1906), *The Kiltartan History Book* (1909), *The Kiltartan Wonder Book* (1910), and the two-volume *Visions and Beliefs in the West of Ireland*, (1920). Of wider impact were *Cuchulain of Muirthemne* (1902) and *Gods and Fighting Men* (1904), in which she compiled, translated, and adaptated the ancient Irish epics so that Ireland would have texts to stand next to Malory's version of the Arthuriad, *Morte D'Arthur*, and the Welsh *Mabinogion.*

It is as a playwright and as a cofounder and the guiding light of the Abbey Theatre that Lady Gregory will be remembered. She wrote twenty-seven original plays, even though she was nearly fifty when she began doing so professionally. Her reputation as a dramatist rests primarily on *Seven Short Plays* (1909) and a few other one-act and two-act comedies. Her longer works, the folk history plays *Kincora* (1905), *Dervorgilla* (1907), and *Grania* (1912), are little regarded today, as are the tragicomedies and few late comedies.

Lady Gregory and the Abbey Theatre are forever linked in Irish cultural history. Not only did she cofound the Irish National Theatre Society and its predecessors; not only did she encourage, support, and defend against nationalists and censors in Ireland and America the first true genius Irish playwright of the twentieth century, John Millington Synge; not only did she discover and encourage that difficult genius Sean O'Casey; not only was she a life-long supporter and best friend of Yeats; but, with magnificent adroitness she kept the Abbey and the company safe from temperamental self-destruction, disastrous elitism, external censorship, political and ecclesiastical control, and Catholic-Protestant rivalry for some thirty years.

Augusta Gregory died at Coole on 22 May 1932. Ireland and the world are forever in her debt.

Plays

Lady Gregory's strengths as a playwright are in the genre of light comedy. Her short, humorous peasant plays still have the power to entertain and delight audiences today and are frequently performed, especially by community and other amateur groups. At the beginning of the twentieth century, she mastered the art of reproducing natural speech and locating dramatic situations in the lives of the common people of Ireland's West. Perhaps an incentive for Lady Gregory was the perceived need to counteract the high seriousness and intense versification in those "literary" plays of Yeats that had limited audience appeal. After all, Lady Gregory had originally hoped that the new Irish theater would tour rural Ireland, putting on plays for the people of the countryside, many of whom would not have seen a professional play before. These relatively unsophisticated people would have related much more comfortably to the stage portraits of people like themselves than to portraits of ancient Celtic chieftains and war goddesses.

Lady Gregory is also good with little plots. She is the inveterate storyteller, bringing a local yarn to life in a very basic, even primeval, way—or, to use the American vernacular, "telling it like it is." She created the mythical village of Coon, based on nearby Gort, as the setting for many of her comedies. A modern reader or viewer might suppose that her naturalist renderings of village and peasant life in a humorous mode are manifestations of aristocratic condescension or colonial perspective: the kindly and sympathetic lady of the manor amused by the machinations of the lower classes or the natives. But I think that we witness in Gregory's comedy, tragicomedy, and miracle and mystery plays precisely what is valorized in her epic adaptations: a drive to establish a delineated Irish character, an Irish collective destiny, an Irish self-recognition, self-respect, and self-understanding.

Lady Gregory's comedies are woven about the themes of illusion and delusion, and appearance versus reality. Characters are fooled, they deceive and trick each other, confusion causes further confusion, and things are never quite what they seem to observers within the plays. Naturally, confusion leads to comic situations and to farcical denouement. Hers is a gentle comedy of manners rather than an acerbic comedy of vice.

Twenty-Five (1903)

Twenty-Five is the story of Christy, a young man who emigrated to America but has returned to his native village with one hundred pounds saved, ostensibly to reclaim his former love, Kate. Significantly, he has been transformed by his overseas experience and, except for Kate, is unrecognized by friends and former neighbors. He proves to be the catalyst that permits others to fulfill their dreams even if he cannot bring his own to life, marriage to Kate, for she has married Michael.

The young family is in financial trouble, and so the generous and loyal Christy arranges to lose the needed fifty pounds, a very considerable sum of money in those days, to Michael in a game of cards called Twenty-Five. Then he departs for America once more, leaving from a community dance, where in farewell to Kate he says: "You wouldn't refuse the greatest stranger in the house. Give me a dance now and I'll be thinking of you sometime when I'm dancing with some high up lady, having golden shoes, in a white marble court by the sea." He leaves with a gallant flourish: a kiss for Kate and a wave of his hat for the neighbors.

Lady Gregory's dialect Irish English is similar to Synge's though not, of course, as metaphorical or lyrical, but the play is six years older than *The Playboy of the Western World*, and surely it paved the way for the ultimate acceptance of Synge's creative diction, if not his plot and character constructs. The Kiltartan dialect of Lady Gregory's country people is never used for disingenuous sentimentality, and there are no Stage Irishmen in her work.

The Rising of the Moon (1903)

The Rising of the Moon is not quite a comedy, but a very short, thrilling one-act play about an Irish rebel escaping from the police. It does have light moments, however. Set on a quay in a seaside town at midnight, the play opens with three policemen looking for a rebel and thinking about the hundred pounds reward. A ballad singer attempts to frighten off the sergeant of the police by warning him that the fugitive is a killer. They sit together, keeping watch, and the singer entertains the policeman with song and the thought that he should attempt to change places in his mind with the rebel. When a boat approaches for the fugitive, a song, "The Rising of the Moon," a rebel song, is heard as the signal. In the end, the sergeant, now sympathetic, helps the fugitive to escape.

Spreading the News (1904)

Recognized as Lady Gregory's little comic masterpiece, *Spreading the News* is her most performed and most anthologized play. The play is based on a misunderstanding that results in a rumor that is embellished as it passes from person to person. No one intends to delude anyone else, but massive misinformation runs rampant because the village people are eager to gossip.

At a country fair Bartley Fallon tries to return a hayfork to his neighbor Jack Smith, who had accidentally left it at the apple stall of Mrs. Tarpey, a woman quite hard of hearing, whose misinterpretations cause much of the mischief of the play. Bartley's wife says that he has gone after Smith with a hayfork—meaning, of course, that he wanted to return it. Mrs. Tarpey then hears that Mrs. Smith is laying out a sheet on a hedge and believes that she has heard "laying out a sheet for the dead." Now people assume that Bartley and Mrs. Smith are having an affair and he wants to do in Smith. A policeman and a magistrate are called in and Bartley is placed under arrest, handcuffed, and charged with murder. His wife berates him and Smith does the same, believing the rumors of the affair. Blunders are amplified. The magistrate, ostensibly an Englishman, is led to believe by misunderstanding the constable that murders frequently occur at the fair. The magistrate often remarks that he has a system for law enforcement:

"When I was in the Andaman Isles my system never failed." Of course, he is not in the Andaman Isles but in the "United" Kingdom of Great Britain and Ireland. To English civil servants, however, one colony is just like another; natives are natives.

Surely Lady Gregory is gently satirizing her deceased husband, that long-serving colonial administrator. In the end Smith is also arrested because he is accused of impersonating the deceased Smith! Poor innocent, well-meaning Bartley, realizing that he may shortly prove to be the corpse, says: "It is what I am thinking, if myself and Jack Smith are put together in the one cell for the night, the handcuffs will be taken off him, and his hands will be free, and murder will be done that time surely!"

In *Spreading the News* the Irish people at the fair say and do funny things, but they are not disparaged or ridiculed by the author. Significantly, here in Lady Gregory's work, as in Synge's, dislike of police is a common underlying assumption about rural Ireland. Although this is comedy, with suspense, surprise, and farcical actions, the characters and situations are still plausible, not absurd, and the audience is left with a feeling of affection for the people of the country fair, a feeling shared with the author. Mild ridicule and satire are directed at the magistrate and the not-too-bright policeman, Joe Muldoon, who has bought into the occupation and distanced himself from the other village people.

Hyacinth Halvey (1906)

A darker and more complex play than *Spreading the News* is *Hyacinth Halvey*, the story of a young man, an assistant sanitary inspector, who comes from Carrow to live in Coon. Because he has come so highly recommended, he has no privacy, living under the constant scrutiny of the parish priest. Furthermore, he is required to perform some difficult and unpleasant duties because he is such a role model. He must wear a teetotaler's button and give morally uplifting lectures to farmers.

Halvey wants fun and his former freedom of action, so he attempts to extricate himself from the restrictive character his letters of recommendation have created. He tries to steal a sheep and fails to do evil because he inadvertently saves the butcher whose tainted meat was to be confiscated. (It is sometimes hard to be bad if one has not had much practice at it.) Then he and his inept accomplice, a messenger boy, attempt to rob a church, but only the boy is accused. Halvey, determined to ruin his reputation, confesses, but the community considers him to be a heroic martyr and even more saintly than before. The cheering crowd, the system—church and state—have him in their stifling embrace forever. He *will* be respectable. The community is all-powerful. The witty play has some of Lady Gregory's most well-crafted dialogue, and Coon springs to life as if she were creating portraiture.

The Jackdaw (1907)

Set in a general store in Coon, *The Jackdaw,* like *The Playboy of the Western World,* indicates the somewhat condescending belief of Anglo-Irish writers like Lady Gregory and Synge that Irish peasants need a hero to worship even if they must construct that person from false information, half-lies, and gossip. Nevertheless *The Jackdaw* is one of Lady Gregory's funniest and most popular plays.

The general store owner is Mrs. Broderick, a middle-aged, illiterate widow who is in debt and nearly bankrupt. She hopes that her well-off brother, Cooney, a farmer near Limerick, will help her, and she has a friend, Joseph Nestor, write letters to him. There are no answers, and the poor woman must go to court. Cooney comes to town and tells Nestor that he wants to help his sister but doesn't want her to know that he is the source of her relief for fear that she will become dependent on him. Cooney is no generous unselfish hero like Christy in *Twenty-Five.*

Lady Gregory seems to be answering her heroic portrait of Christy with that of the pragmatic, loss-cutting Cooney, whose name seems to symbolize the people of the area. Nestor fabricates a wild yarn about an Irish-born South African mine owner who is lonely for Ireland and wants the company of an Irish bird that is able to survive in a dark mine. Only one bird fits the bill: the jackdaw, a bird that lives in chimneys. The mine owner supposedly has sent ten pounds through an agent to pay for one. Mrs. Broderick is given Cooney's much-needed money for her pet jackdaw. But Cooney actually believes Nestor's concocted story, too, and goes off to an old mill looking for more jackdaws to sell.

Unwilling to tell people how she got the ten pounds, Mrs. Broderick sees her reputation in the community slipping and attacks Cooney for not finding a bird to deliver to the imaginary agent. Meanwhile everyone in the village from the magistrate on down goes on a bird hunt, looking for jackdaws to sell to the "agent." Although she has the money, Mrs. Broderick refuses to believe that it came from her brother and is unsatisfied: "Satisfied is it? It would be a queer thing indeed I to be satisfied. My brother to be spending money on birds, and his sister with a summons on her head." At the end the fatuous police force is searching for the missing "agent," the principals are afraid they will be arrested for a nonexistent crime, and the audience is left laughing at the unending farce.

Nestor, named after the wise old Greek, has been made a local hero solely because he is a learned man and can spin a good yarn. He is more like the merrygreek of early Renaissance English comedy, bent on clever mischief, a character itself derived from the wily slave of Roman comedy. Nestor does not deserve their adulation, of course, and so the play gently satirizes the gullibility of the West Country folk.

The Gaol Gate (1908)

A very short curtain-raiser tragedy, *The Gaol Gate* shows West Country peasant hatred for British law and the informers who kept the system going. In the play two women visit a jail where a man—son and husband—is held as an informer. Upon arrival they are told that the man has died. They are sad that he will have the bad name of an informer. When they are given his clothes and told that he was hanged, it is good news for them and they rejoice because he would not have been hanged if he had informed. Their kin is not a traitor after all; he gave his life for Ireland. Lady Augusta is preaching self-sacrifice of the individual for the sake of the oppressed community. She had become a literary rebel herself.

The Workhouse Ward (1908)

Originally called *The Poorhouse* and based on Lady Gregory's knowledge of the workhouse in Gort, the comedy satirizes Irish pretentiousness and absurd pride as evidenced in two sickly, old, indigent men, ancient antagonists and once feuding neighbors, who now continue the feud from adjoining beds. Each one claims finer lineage and higher status than the other. When the sister of one of the men arrives with a suit of clothes to take him out of the workhouse, he refuses to go without his old enemy, to whom he is sentimentally attached. The sister wants only one man—as cheap labor—not two, and so she starts to leave with the suit, but the old men speed her departure by pelting her with everything they can lay their hands on. Lady Gregory saw in the Irish character a great need for community and a deep-seated craving for talk; it is better to have someone to argue with than to be alone.

The Full Moon (1910)

In *The Full Moon*, Lady Gregory, as if to draw her comedies into a folk cycle, employs in this play a host of characters from earlier plays, such as Bartley Fallon from *Spreading the News*, Mrs. Broderick from *The Jackdaw*, Hyacinth Halvey, and others.

Halvey supposedly has been bitten by a mad dog: "as big as a calf . . . a milch cow. . . . Terrible wicked he is; he's as big as five dogs, and he does be very strong." (The animal in fact is small, tame, and safe.) The people of Coon believe the rumor and, afraid that they will be bitten by him, attempt to chain him, just as the Mayo people in *The Playboy of the Western World* jump and tie up Christy Mahon, the seemingly mad-dog parricide, near the end of the play. In the end Halvey escapes, realizing that he did not have to live among the "insane" people of Coon, the sanest of whom is Cracked Mary, the former resident of the local madhouse.

The Bogie Man (1912)

A well-constructed two-character play, *The Bogie Man* is set at a coach stop where two impoverished chimney sweeps meet. As neither is happy to run into "one of my own trade," each one boasts to the other about his affluent first cousin, a paragon of virtue and a most competent and able youth—in other words, an impossible role model. Each is boasting so as to appear to be of a higher social position than the other. As the boys change their clothes and wash the chimney black off their faces, they recognize each other. They are the cousins. Good-naturedly they assert that they will never weave untrue fantasies again to make themselves more important than they are. Moreover, they are going to be pals. The audience enjoys both the early moment of recognition, when it first realizes that the lads must each be the cousin awaited by the other, and the second moment of recognition when the characters learn the same.

Darner's Gold (1912)

Lady Gregory's miser play is indebted to Molière's *L'Avarice* (*The Miser*), which in turn is based on Plautus's *Aulularia* (*The Pot of Gold*). Darner, a miser, has a gallon jug nearly full of gold coins that is his pride and joy. Darner's brother, his niece Delia, and her husband enter Darner's home and discuss his miserliness while he, in hiding, eavesdrops on them. He refuses any attempt by them to make his home more livable because it would require spending money.

In act 2 the miser changes, becoming generous and charitable, and begins to enjoy life. His relatives, especially Delia, think he has gone mad and plan how to spend his money. But Darner has lost his money playing cards with a man named Simon, who turns out to be a nephew in disguise. The other relatives are frustrated as the former miser and his pleasure-loving nephew, now strongly bonded, go off to enjoy the money. Like Molière, Lady Gregory applauds generosity and those who take pleasure in life. As a wealthy aristocrat who was also a generous person, Lady Gregory felt she was in a position to chastise the greedy Delias of the villages and countryside.

Hanrahan's Oath (1917)

A slight comedy, *Hanrahan's Oath* is about a garrulous poet, Hanrahan, whose name is taken from Yeats's stories in *The Celtic Twilight,* and who is possibly based on Yeats. Hanrahan believes that because he talks too much, he has informed on his friend who has kept an illegal still. He vows an oath of silence, and people think he is a holy man, until he learns that his friend has not been convicted and he becomes garrulous again.

A widow, Mary Gillis, a rooming-house owner, with whom Hanrahan has been lodging, may have been a humorous self-portrait by Lady Gregory. Mary Gillis tries to trick Hanrahan into staying with her, but the poet leaves her with a curse as he goes off with a young woman named Margaret Rooney. In the same year as the production of the play, Yeats married a very young and affluent Englishwoman, Miss Bertha Georgie Hyde-Lees, and seemed to be about to desert Ireland for life in England. *Hanrahan's Oath* may have been Lady Gregory's way of dealing with what she thought was the loss of a dear friend. Fortunately, the friendship endured for the rest of her life.

Additional Reading

Gregory, Lady Isabella Augusta. *Our Irish Theatre.* 1913. Reprint, Gerrards Cross, England: Colin Smythe, 1972.

――――. *Selected Plays of Lady Gregory.* Washington, D.C.: Catholic University of America Press, 1983.

Kohfeldt, Mary Lou. *Lady Gregory: The Woman Behind the Irish Renaissance.* New York: Atheneum. 1985.

Saddlemyer, Anne. *In Defence of Lady Gregory, Playwright.* Dublin: Dolmen, 1966.

William Butler Yeats

(1865–1939)

William Butler Yeats, was Ireland's greatest poet and arguably the leading poet of the English language in the twentieth century, became as large a legend as any ancient hero he sang about. In a lifetime of genius and creativity, his poetry continued to mutate, develop, extend, and grow in profundity and power. As *the* poet of the new Irish nation, he made Ireland and things Irish culturally fashionable in the marketplace of the English-speaking world.

Additionally, Yeats was the prime mover of and major spokesperson for the Irish Literary Revival, an essayist, an autobiographer, a mystic, an Irish senator, an ardent opponent of censorship, and a proponent of free artistic expression, the 1923 recipient of the Nobel Prize for Literature, and of course, a founder of the National Theatre Society.

Yeats, the author of two dozen plays, always thought of himself as a dramatist too—perhaps primarily. He was a playwright of importance, and, as a founder and codirector of the Abbey and its predecessor for more than half of his lifetime, he helped make Dublin for the first twenty-five or thirty of the twentieth century a theater capital equal in originality, profundity, and creativity to any city in Europe or the Americas. He made a contribution to Irish and European culture that remains a source of great pleasure and pride in Ireland, and he was a foundation for so much out-standing literary achievement that came later in Ireland and is still happening.

Yeats's creative life has two great psychological secrets. First, he was a counterrevolutionary, intellectually and emotionally battling his father, who was himself in revolt against the values of the Victorian age. Second, he was always mindful of the fact that he was the son of the Irish bourgeoisie, clergy and business peo-ple, not the landed gentry, and he aspired to be accepted by or even become one of the latter.

Born in Dublin, William Butler Yeats was the eldest of four surviving children in a talented Protestant family headed by the fine portrait painter, raconteur, and impractical husband-father, John Butler Yeats, and the quiet, sensitive Sligo-reared, Sligo-lov-ing, ever-worrying mother, Susan Pollexfen. "Willy" spent his early childhood in Sligo, while John Butler Yeats, previously trained as a lawyer at Trinity College, Dublin, studied painting in London. Yeats's siblings also grew up to be artists; his brother Jack B. Yeats became one of Ireland's most renowned painters.

Young William was taken from beautiful Sligo to London, along with the rest of his family, so that all could live together again with his father. Yeats studied at the Godolphin School in Hammersmith. When the Yeats family moved back to Dublin in 1880, William attended the High School, Harcourt Street. His fa-ther wanted his firstborn son to attend Trinity College, Dublin, as he had, but Yeats, a poor student, never could have passed the en-trance exam, and so he chose the Metropolitan School of Art and then the Royal Hibernian Academy. There he became a lifelong friend of George Russell, the poet AE, and Russell introduced him to fellow mystics, beginning Yeats's fascination with the occult.

It must be pointed out that Yeats's childhood, adolescence, and early manhood years were lived against the defeats and re-treat of his class and the class he admired, the Protestant middle class and the Protestant Anglo-Irish Ascendancy. The Land Acts and the Land War weakened landowners' control, in jumps and starts, Home Rule—if not full independence—was coming. Surely these events that his father supported (but the rest of his family did not) helped turn Yeats's thought and then his art towards the romantic and safely dead Irish past.

In 1886 he decided on a writing career instead of one in the fine arts, and he began producing poetry based on English models and without Irish content. Then, under the influence of the old Fenian fighter John O'Leary, Yeats turned to Irish subjects and themes.

• • •

The Yeats family went back to London in 1887. There Yeats met Madame Helena Blavatsky and joined the Theosophists and the Order of the Golden Dawn. Yeats would later state that the mystical life was central "to all that I think and all that I write." In 1891, Yeats was one of the founders of the Rhymers' Club in London. Yeats also became active in the literary politics of Irish writers in London, founding the Irish Literary Society of London in 1891 and in 1892, with other people, the National Literary Society, an organization to promulgate the literature, mythology, legend, and folklore of Ireland. Yeats's contribution to the movement, and his first literary success, was his long mythological poem *The Wanderings of Oisín* (1889). Four years later another major publication, *The Celtic Twilight*, showed both his growing skill in prose and his ability to turn folklore into very readable material for the contemporary public.

In 1889, Yeats met the great love of his life, the beautiful Maude Gonne. His painful, unrequited love for her would be a source of both inspiration and intense pain for Yeats for much of his life, because Maude Gonne refused him again and again. Gonne made Yeats over into a republican, and under her influence he joined the Irish Republican Brotherhood and began to be more active politically.

According to her diary, Lady Gregory and Yeats first met in

the spring of 1894, the same year that his first stage production, *The Land of Heart's Desire*, played in London. The wealthy, aristocratic woman became his most important friend, and their mutual influence was of incalculable significance to them and to Irish culture. Spending many summers at Coole Park with Lady Gregory, Yeats found the calm, security, and natural beauty he needed in order to write some of his finest lyrics and plays.

As I discussed earlier, the idea of an Irish theater came into existence in September 1897, at the end of the very first summer Yeats spent at Coole, when Yeats and Lady Gregory met with her neighbor, Edward Martyn of Tulira Castle, at Duras House, County Galway. The next year they founded the Irish Literary Theatre, forerunner of the Irish National Theatre Society, the Abbey. In 1899, Yeats's first production in Ireland, *The Countess Cathleen*, starring Florence Farr, was performed in Dublin. The second, *Diarmuid and Grania*, was a failed collaboration with the novelist George Moore in 1901.

Earlier, while still residing in London, Yeats visited Paris and met John Millington Synge in 1896. Their friendship endured for the rest of Synge's short life. Yeats urged Synge to stop trying to be a French Symbolist writer and return to Ireland to study peasant life, searching Irish roots for subject, theme, and language. Synge did, to the glory of Irish drama.

In 1902, Yeats returned to Ireland and became president of the National Theatre Society. His *Cathleen ni Houlihan* starred Maude Gonne that year. The next year Yeats made the first of several lecture tours of the United States. In 1903 his poetry collection *In the Seven Woods* appeared.

At the Abbey's first performance in 1904, Yeats's *On Baile's Strand*, one of his finest plays and the first of five dramas based on the legend of the epic hero Cuchulain, was on the bill. The next year *The King's Threshold* was on the boards. *Poems, 1899–1905* was published in 1906, the same year that *Deidre* was first performed at the Abbey. Two years later Ezra Pound met Yeats, becoming an ardent admirer and even Yeats's secretary for a short period. Pound introduced Yeats to Japanese Noh drama, and thus influenced his later play-writing, because Yeats found himself fascinated with the Noh's use of masks, symbols, and ritual dancing. Yeats continued to write poetry and plays prolifically, publishing *The Green Helmet and Other Poems* in 1910, the same year his name appeared on the British Civil List for an annual pension of 150 pounds per annum.

The next year, in England, Yeats met his future wife, the nineteen-year-old Miss Bertha Georgie Hyde-Lees, later affectionately known as George. They would keep in touch and then marry six years later. When his friend and protégé Synge died in 1909, Yeats edited the younger writer's *Poems and Translations* as a memorial act of friendship and homage.

In 1903, Maude Gonne had married Major John MacBride, who had fought the British in the Boer War. The marriage was not a happy one. But MacBride was, like Gonne, an Irish patriot, and he was one of the leaders of the 1916 Easter Uprising, for which he was executed by the British government. Yeats, a supporter of the failed rebellion, wrote several poems in honor of the martyrs.

But Yeats's mind was also on starting a family, belated though the thought was. Thus he purchased Thoor Ballylee, a decrepit medieval Norman tower near Coole, County Galway, which he had first seen when walking with Lady Gregory years before. His plan was to marry and bring his bride to Thoor Ballylee; he would renovate the tower, creating a summer home for the family and a place in which he could communicate with the spirits of the past and the stars in the night heavens. Maude Gonne turned him down again, and the following year, smitten by her daughter Iseult, he proposed marriage to her, but she too rejected Yeats. George, now twenty-five (Yeats, fifty-two), was next on the list, and she said yes. A daughter, Anne Butler Yeats, was born in 1919, and a son, William Michael Yeats, in 1921.

Meanwhile the poetry collection *Responsibilities* appeared in 1914, the play *At the Hawk's Well* was produced in London in 1916,

The Wild Swans at Coole was published in 1917, and *Michael Robartes and the Dancer* was published in 1920. With the Anglo-Irish War and then the Irish Civil War raging, Yeats, who supported the treaty establishing the Irish Free State and was opposed to the Irish Republican Army rebelling against the new Irish government, spent more time in England than in Ireland, either in Dublin or Ballylee, for the safety of his family. He finally established a central Dublin residence, 82 Merrion Square in 1922, the year he became a member of the Irish Senate, and just before the world recognition that came with the Nobel Prize for Literature the next year. In 1922, *Four Plays for Dancers* appeared in print.

Yeats adapted Sophocles's *Oedipus Rex,* and the play was performed at the Abbey in 1926. Still considered the outstanding poetic and dramatically playable translation of the ancient Greek classic, it is also frequently read as a school text. It was brilliantly performed by the Canadian Shakespeare Festival at Stratford, Ontario, many seasons ago in a production directed by the Festival founder Tyrone Guthrie and presented with masks. Yeats's adaptation of Sophocles's *Oedipus at Colonus* (1934) has proved less popular.

Also in 1926, Yeats helped to design the new Irish coinage; several of the animal designs are still being used on today's decimal coins. The memorable poetry collection inspired by Thoor Ballylee, *The Tower,* was published in 1928.

In the last decade of his life, Yeats moved between London, Dublin, and Ballylee and Coole Park in Galway. In 1932, the year his dear friend Lady Gregory died, the Yeatses moved from Merrion Square to Riversdale, Rathfarnham, County Dublin. This was his final residence in the country of his birth.

With George Bernard Shaw and AE (George Russell), Yeats founded the Irish Academy of Letters in 1932. *The Winding Stair and Other Poems* appeared in 1933, along with *Collected Poems; Collected Plays* in 1934; and a Salome play, *A Full Moon in March,* was published in 1935. Yeats's creativity, especially in poetry, continued throughout his life.

Yeats had worked on his autobiography (which really does not tell the reader all that much about his actual life) in installments: *Reveries over Childhood and Youth* (1915), *The Trembling of the Veil* (1922), and *Dramatis Personae* (1936).

With his health failing, Yeats went to warm his ailing body on the French Riviera in the winter of 1938. Visits to the South of France in winters past had been beneficial; this time he died—at Roquebrune, near Monaco, on 28 January 1939. He was temporarily buried there, but World War II prevented his body being returned to Ireland until 1948, when an Irish warship brought his remains to his beloved Sligo, and he was buried in Drumcliffe churchyard, next to the parish church that once had been his grandfather's. Yeats had always wanted to be buried in sight of the great Sligo mountain—"under bare Ben Bulben's head." He had written his instructions for an epitaph:

> No marble, no conventional phrase;
> On limestone quarried near the spot
> By his command these words are cut:
>   Cast a cold eye
>   On life, on death
>   Horseman, pass by!

They were so cut on limestone. But Yeats had not cast a cold eye on life. His had been warm, full, and graced with love, friendship, respect, and the power to move people and, indeed, a nation.

George devoted much of the rest of her life to the task of being the family archivist. She died in 1968.

Plays

William Butler Yeats was a passionate man who used passionate language. He saw in drama the possibility of depicting the irreconcilable, irresolvable conflicts of life. He believed in the greatness of the human spirit and soul, and a greatness that was best manifested by noble action under tragic situations. Human greatness was a symbol on earth of God's greatness.

Yeats always attempted to concoct a unique brew of symbol and scene, sound and sense, ritual and reality, and action and thought. Myths and archetypes, those mind capsules of eternal truths, were the primary means by which Yeats communicated his passion and intensity to his audience. Although a mythomane, Yeats also wrote peasant plays (with the help of Lady Gregory), but his heart was with those of his characters based on folk legends and Irish mythology. Looking at the totality of his dramatic work, one quickly realizes that Yeats was an innovator, an experimentalist, and a ritualist in style and dramaturgy. His favorite themes were those that emphasized heroic action and noble sacrifice. He knew as well as anyone else that romantic Ireland was dead and gone, but his commitment to lyricism and his love of beauty put him at odds with Ibsenites determined to show the poverty and sordidness of rural and urban contemporary Irish life. To Yeats, Ireland was a beautiful queen, not the old, grasping, bigoted hag that other writers, realists and naturalists, sometimes saw.

For Yeats, writing drama was something of a priestly occupation, and the theater was a sacred place of mystery and patriotism. Not surprisingly, he called some of his dramas mystery or morality plays. And Yeats learned from Sophocles that inner conflict reflects conflict in God's universe—weeping for order. In his drama Yeats reached for the divinity that is within humankind, finding it in heroes and heroines who move, like Plato's shadows, in conjunction with the prototypes of our spiritual world. Thus for Yeats character is destiny and destiny is within character.

The Cuchulain Saga

Between 1903 and the last week of his life, Yeats wrote five plays on the life, exploits, and death of his favorite epic hero from the Ulster Cycles, Cuchulain: *On Baile's Strand* (1904), *The Green*

Helmet (1910), *At the Hawks Well* (1916), *The Only Jealousy of Emer* (written 1919, performed 1922), and *The Death of Cuchulain* (1939). One might surmise that Yeats was especially proud of his one epic dramatic cycle.

On Baile's Strand

Yeats wrote *On Baile's Strand* as if he were an Irish Sophocles. His hero is brought to his fall by the flaws of his character, pride and rashness, as well as by his fate. His final struggle, a mad battle with the sea, is perhaps Yeats's adaptation of that Quixotic courage in the Irish character that in Irish history led to so many glorious defeats at the hands of overwhelming invaders.

The heroic warrior Cuchulain, the man of passion and action, at first opposes the clever, crafty High King Conchubar, but the king is skilled at manipulation, and finally the hero submits, takes an oath, and as a pledge must kill in combat a certain brave young man. His intuition tries to restrain him, and he wants to befriend the young man, but it is to no avail. The king forces the combat, and Cuchulain slays the youth, who turns out to be his own son, the product of the brief, youthful affair with the warrior queen Aoife—a son of whose existence he was unaware. The intelligent but passionless and heartless Conchubar has orchestrated everything in order to preserve the succession of his own sons. Cuchulain cannot fathom or accept his tragic fate. He has no son to carry on his name; just as he believed before he knew of the life and caused the death of his only son, he will be remembered only by the harp. Thus in madness he marches into the army of waves, striking them with his sword as he is overwhelmed by the sea.

Like Greek tragedy, *On Baile's Strand* is written in verse and employs a chorus of women for intensification, and heroic speeches from the oral tradition, for the rituals of historical identification and confrontation. A thieving blind man and a singing fool, both in masks, symbolize the craftiness of the king and the passionate love of life of the hero. The play is a superb welding of symbol, archetype, and action—a work of great aesthetic beauty.

The Green Helmet

The lightest of Yeats's Cuchulain dramas, *The Green Helmet*, has comedy as well as drama, and the hero is presented at his most magnanimous, committed to joie de vivre. His generous and noble conduct is meant to contrast with the meanness Yeats saw in his contemporary Ireland. The play is structured around three episodes, each employing the same characters but having its own denouement. In the beginning a beheading challenge and the presence of the Green Helmet agitate the warriors. Three warriors fight over the right to wear the Green Helmet, a possession and an action denoting precedence, and Cuchulain resolves the conflict by filling the helmet with ale and having the warriors drink equally, thus symbolizing their equality and friendship. Then he flings the trouble-causing helm into the sea.

In the second episode each of three great ladies, all wives of heroes, wishes to enter the banqueting hall first, because each believes her husband is the greatest hero and therefore she deserves primacy of place among the wives. Like Solomon or Odysseus, wise Cuchulain solves the dilemma by not letting his own wife, Emer, enter before the other two women have broken passages in the wall, so that all parties may enter simultaneously. Face is saved, and vanity served.

Finally Cuchulain offers himself as a pledge for the honor of his people when the red man comes to take Cuchulain's life. Instead, he presents Cuchulain with the Green Helmet. He is the greatest of the heroes, ready to defend his right to the honor of being the champion.

The satire on the human frailties and vanities of the heroes and their wives is quite amusing, and it gives the play a realism and an earthiness that the other Cuchulain dramas do not contain.

At the Hawk's Well

One of Yeats's most beautiful plays, *At the Hawk's Well*, explores the possibilities of the Noh dramatic tradition employed in the service of Irish legend. The powerful, energy-filled drama uses masks, drum, gong, zither, highly stylized dancing that is simultaneously modern and ancient, an especially significant and aesthetically satisfying chorus, and some of Yeats's finest dramatic imagery.

Although the third Cuchulain play written by Yeats, *The Hawk's Well* precedes all the others in the order of the epic. Here the young, headstrong, confident Cuchulain is initiated into his role as signifier of a culture and a history. He comes to the Hawk's Well to drink from the magical water so that he may become godlike—immortal, passionate, and creative—but is confronted by the guardian of the well, a crafty supernatural woman who tricks him from his purpose by luring him into the woods, seemingly for seduction, but then disappears.

Cuchulain, unable to couple with the immortal, must satisfy himself with living flesh. This is appropriate and natural for a youth of his age; the young must always choose the pleasure and the purpose of the temporal world. Unbeknownst to him, his sexual encounter with Aoife, sets the stage for the most tragic episode in his saga, for she is to be the vengeful mother of the son he will slay one day. Although Cuchulain is defeated in his attempt to capture the waters of immortality, he exults in the realization that his destiny is to live: to thrive not in the supernatural world but in the world of human passion, desire, and frailty. Cuchulain's character contrasts with that of the old man living by the well for fifty years who is satisfied with the most meager portion of life: Cuchulain intuitively understands that the length of one's life is not what is significant; it is the passion and range of experience of a life that marks its value.

The Only Jealousy of Emer

The Only Jealousy of Emer is one of the group Yeats titled *Four Plays for Dancers*. They are written in the Noh style with music and highly ritualistic and symbolic movement by dancers. In *The Only Jealousy of Emer*, Cuchulain is a shadowy, dreaming figure recalling the past with remorse. The play begins with a melancholy lyric about the frailty and the glory of a woman's beauty. Next, in a fisherman's cottage, Cuchulain lies in a trance. He has been brought from the strand and is near death. His wife, Emer, summons his mistress, Eithne, to his bedside to attempt to return him to life, a deed Emer is unable to do.

The Only Jealousy of Emer is a verse play of marriage and the ancient triangle of lust and jealousy: husband, wife, his lover. Cuchulain dreams on, and then Eithne woos him back to the land of the living. Masks are used to present the many, complex sides of character. The darker faces of Cuchulain drive the mistress from his side, but the wife must see all sides of the husband, even his low, unreachable ghost-spirit. Yet—and above all—Emer wishes to regain the love of her husband, but heroically she is willing to forego that forever if it will bring back the old spirit of the hero she loves. She moves beyond jealousy to sacrifice. He will awake but never in her arms. The married couple communicate on the deepest level with few words but with the feeling and understanding that comes from long, familiar love.

The Death of Cuchulain

The dying Yeats and the dying Cuchulain finally merge in Yeats's last play—or, at the least, Yeats "signs" his epic plays by having one character, an old man, refer to "the old epics and Mr. Yeats' plays about them."

As Cuchulain moves toward death, his wife, the wise Emer, attempts to prevent the old hero from battling the offspring of the witch Calatin, because Emer knows that the old hero is unable to defeat their power of enchantment, but Calatin's one-eyed daughter Badh provokes him. Another daughter, The Moorage, Irish goddess of war, attempts to prevent the hero from engaging in the battle by damaging his war chariot, but to no avail. Cuchulain will not be detained. In the fierce battle he is mortally wounded, leaves the field to find water, ties himself to a standing stone, and is killed and beheaded by the blind man of *On Baile's Strand*. The plays are linked. Emer mourns, and the warrior Conall revenges. Yeats has rounded up all the old cast of the Cuchulain cycle in *The Death of Cuchulain*: Queen Maeve, Emer, the vengeful Aoife, the mistress Eithne, and others for the grand finale, and with it the cycle of Cuchulain is over. Was the hero's "life" of passionate action the life Yeats himself had longed for?

Other Mythic Plays

The Shadowy Waters (1904)

Forgael, the poet-harpist-hero, abducts Dectora from her husband, King Iollan, who is killed. Dectora attempts to command her abductor and his men, but Forgael prevents her. Forgael is transformed or reborn as her rightful husband and king, and they are joined in immortal love. Forgael stands for human intellect and reason, and Dectora represents sexuality. The story is a human one raised to the divine by sublime poetry.

Deidre (1906)

Despite the fact that it is based on the world-beloved story of the love of Deidre and Naoise, the Irish equivalent of the tale of Tristan and Iseult, the tragedy of *Deidre* does not succeed. Yeats had not yet assimilated the values and the power of Sophoclean tragedy. It is Synge who brings dramatic passion and life to the great love story later in his *Deidre of the Sorrows*. Nevertheless, the character of Deidre is beautifully portrayed by Yeats. Again a warrior king—this time Conchubar—loses the love and the possession of his young bride to a younger man. The king is the old, crafty bourgeois; Naoise is the brave man of action. In the ensuing battle Naoise is made prisoner and ignominiously executed. Again youth is denied its natural triumph. Deidre cannot live without young love. With her concealed knife she takes her own life to join her lover in death.

Political Plays

Cathleen ni Houlihan (1902)

Yeats's most famous and most frequently performed play, *Cathleen ni Houlihan*, is one of those works of art that influence history. Long after the first performance, and after young men had died in the Easter 1916 attempt to free Ireland from British rule, Yeats considered what he had wrought: "Did that play of mine send out/Certain young men the English Shot?" ("The Man and the Echo"). The words are famous, the question more than rhetorical. Yeats and other early dramatists did inspire the patriotism that first led to failure and then to success.

Set in a cottage in the West in 1798, the fateful year of a failed Irish revolt, a poor, old, peasant woman, Cathleen ni Houlihan, who symbolizes Ireland, convinces Michael Gillane to leave his fiancée and his comfortable life to join other Irish people and the invading French to fight the English for the freedom of the nation. He rushes from his lover's arms and dashes out at the call of Cathleen. The last words of the play are spoken by Michael's father ("Did you see an old woman going down the path?") and his son Patrick ("I did not, but I saw a young girl, and she had the walk of a queen."). Ireland can be transformed from poor peasant to beautiful queen only by the dedication and brave sacrifices of her young.

The Dreaming of the Bones (1931, first published 1919)

A dance play based on Noh dramaturgy and style, *The Dreaming of the Bones* presents a confrontation between the ghosts of the past, Diarmuid and Dervorgilla, who were the royal pair responsible for bringing the Norman conquest and English rule to Ireland in the twelfth century, and a young Irish revolutionary who fought with Ireland's heroes at the Post Office during the Easter Rising of 1916. Diarmuid and Dervorgilla are tortured by the knowledge that they betrayed their race. Only forgiveness from one of their race can end their agony, but the young man cannot find it in his heart to do so. He could forgive almost anyone, but not these traitors. The play ends with Diarmuid and Dervorgilla performing a Dantean dance of penance and remorse.

Purgatory (1938)

Another ghost story, *Purgatory*, is a Greek-like tale of the need to purify a family from the sin that began its curse. An old man, a peddler of the West at the ruins of Castle Dargan near Sligo, informs his son about the history of the derelict house. Ghosts of the house appear. The boy and the father fight over paltry money, and the boy is slain with the knife his father had used against his grandfather.

These mean men represent the Irish of Yeats's present, and the castle ruins signify his ruined nation, split and tortured by continual dissension and division. The murder replicates past manifestations of the curse. The play ends with the old man praying that God will let the dead be still and will end the sufferings of the living. But it is only after the passion has burned out that Purgatory may be escaped. Compact, sparse, and tight, the play succeeds on both the level of political allegory and that of generational tragedy.

Folk and Fairy-Tale Plays

The Countess Cathleen (1899)

Yeats revised *The Countess Cathleen* again and again—in 1901, 1912, 1919—and also made slight changes from time to time. Clearly, he saw in the character of the countess a personification of the noble Irish nation—someone who would do anything, make any sacrifice, for the people.

Opposing the attempts of two demon-merchants to buy the souls of the starving peasants, the countess sells her own soul to them to save her people. (Although the poet Kevin has tried to sell his soul to prevent Cathleen from selling hers, his effort is in vain.) However, because the countess is pure and saintly, her soul does not go to hell, but instead goes to heaven, where it is welcomed with great joy as the play ends. Through self-sacrifice she has defeated the forces of evil. Subsequent versions of the play are more complex, but the initial, simpler text seems to play best.

The Pot of Broth (1902)

This play, so reminiscent of Lady Gregory's subjects and style, is one of Yeats's very few comedies. Using simple and direct dialect language, the short play has a nameless tramp as hero—actually, anti-hero, because he lives by his wits and his words as he cadges for his daily bread. He shows a "magic" stone to an avaricious woman, Sibey Coneely, and gets her to put food into the pot with the stew-providing stone. The foolish woman is saved from further duping only by the imminent arrival of the parish priest and thus the quick retreat of the clever tramp. *The Pot of Broth* affirms the freedom of the road and the triumph of wit over the bourgeois values of those with fixed abodes and materialistic visions. The plot is related to the Russian folk tale "Stone Soup."

The Hour-Glass (1903, 1914)

Yeats chose to rewrite this play extensively ten years after its first production, changing the dialogue, converting prose to verse, and adding some of the experimental staging he had embraced in his career as a dramatist. It is the rewritten version with masks that is usually studied and occasionally performed. *The Hour-Glass* is a morality play and allegory like *Everyman*. The Wise Man finds salvation through humbling himself to the Fool, Teigue. An angel causes him to change his arrogant ways. Yeats wants the skeptical intelligentsia of his time to accept the possibility of miracles. The "fools" of the world are the holy people who believe—who are connected to the reality of the spiritual. The road to salvation for the "wise" is to accept God's will completely.

The King's Threshold (1903)

Yeats evidences his concern for the role of the poet and artist in society in *The King's Threshold*. He also advances the concept of the ideal hero-citizen: a combination of sensitive poet and person of action. The society that neglects the artist's role is tragically handicapped. Seanchan, the passionate bard, is also a man of action. His antagonist, the king, is a political creature, a man of reason, and a materialist.

There is a general conspiracy to corrupt Seanchan and deprive him of his idealism. Church, state, and army work on him. Though tempted by flattery, love, beauty, and sex, he does not succumb. The poet-hero goes to his death (by hunger strike) undaunted and safe in his convictions, an example for all.

Additional Reading

Ellmann, Richard. *Yeats: The Man and the Masks.* New York: Macmillan, 1948.

Foster, Roy. *W. B. Yeats. A Life.* Vol.1, *The Apprentice Mage.* London: Oxford Univ. Press, 1997.

Taylor, Richard. *A Reader's Guide to the Plays of W. B. Yeats.* New York: St. Martin's, 1984.

Unterecker, John. *A Reader's Guide to William Butler Yeats.* New York: Noonday, 1959; reprint, Syracuse, N.Y.: Syracuse Univ. Press, 1996.

Yeats, William Butler. *The Collected Plays of W. B. Yeats.* New York: Macmillan, 1953.

———. *Eleven Plays of William Butler Yeats.* Edited by Norman A. Jeffares. New York: Macmillan, 1964.

George Bernard Shaw
(1856–1950)

Like his fellow Dublin-born playwright Oscar Wilde (1854–1900), George Bernard Shaw had a distinctly Irish wit but made his contribution to the drama and the theater in England. He is represented here, but relatively briefly, because of his one full-length play about Ireland, the controversial *John Bull's Other Island* (the very title could raise a republican's temperature ten degrees.)

Shaw was born into the Protestant lower-middle class, the one son and third child of a heavy-drinking, continually failing merchant named George Carr Shaw, and Elizabeth Gurly Shaw, a woman who had pretentions to a career as a singer. Her music teacher, George Vandeleur Lee, moved into the house on Upper Synge Street (33 Synge Street) and formed the other leg of a marital triangle. Shaw received a secondary education at Wesley College but could not attend Trinity College, Dublin because of lack of funds. What amounted to his higher education came partly through the music that he heard at home, as well as from his many hours of reading and his study of pictures in the National Gallery. At sixteen he was a clerk in a business office. When the music teacher left for London, Mrs. Shaw followed.

Shaw was left with his father for four years, and then in 1876 he joined his mother and her lover in London, where she supported him while he wrote one unsuccessful novel after another. Shaw did not return to Ireland for nearly thirty years. For nine years of literary effort he earned almost nothing. Moved by the plight of London's poor, he joined the Fabian Society and became an effective speaker for socialism. William Archer, the drama critic and theorist, found Shaw work as a book reviewer. He also became a music critic.

Shaw turned to play writing in 1892 with his attack on slumlords, *Widowers' Houses*. Other plays followed, including *Mrs. Warren's Profession*, *Arms and the Man*, and *Candida*, but his first success was *The Devil's Disciple*, followed by *Man and Superman*, *Major Barbara*, and *Pygmalion*. In 1898, Shaw married an affluent Anglo-Irish woman, Charlotte Payne-Townshend. Joining with the producer-playwright Harley Granville-Barker at the Royal Court Theatre, Shaw became Britain's leading playwright.

At Yeats's request, Shaw wrote *John Bull's Other Island* for the Irish Literary Theatre, but the controversial play was not shown in Dublin until much later. During World War I, Shaw was an ardent and vociferous pacifist, and he was blackballed and nearly imprisoned. Fame returned after the war, with such plays as *Heartbreak House* and *St. Joan*; he received the Nobel Prize for Literature in 1925. The Shaws had no children, and Charlotte Shaw died in 1943. He continued writing up to his death in 1950.

Shaw was an Ibsenite. He took Henrik Ibsen's concept of the thesis play—in which a problem of middle-class society is presented for consideration by the society itself, as represented by the audience—and employed it in social comedies that sparkled with wit and wonderful dialogue. Without doubt, Shaw is the greatest playwright of the English language since Shakespeare. His only possible challenger is that very different master of Existentialist drama, Samuel Beckett, who will be discussed later.

His Irish Play: *John Bull's Other Island* (1904)

In typical Shavian fashion, *John Bull's Other Island* inverts the expected cliché: the play's chief and typical Englishman, Tom

Broadbent, is the sentimentalist, gushing over monastic ruins and the peasant life, while the play's chief Irishman, Larry Doyle, is a hard-headed realist, critical of Irish values and self-delusion, without sentiment for Irish ways or Irish women. Although Broadbent is sentimental about old Ireland, he is of course a great business person, who will make a substantial profit from Ireland, marry the girl who has been waiting years for the indecisive Doyle, and actually get to represent an Irish constituency in the British parliament because the Irish people would rather be represented by a free-wheeling, malarkey-spreading Briton than one of their own. Shaw thus satirizes both the English middle-class professional who seems such a role model for the Irish and the middle-class Irishman who makes his living in England and out of admiration has become more English than the English.

The plot of the play centers on the conquest of an Irish village, Rosscullen, by Tom Broadbent, an English engineer. This conquest is a symbolic microcosm of the relationship between England and Ireland as Shaw saw it at the turn of the twentieth century, and as many Irish people still see it today—thus the continued interest in the play. Broadbent's Irish partner, Larry Doyle, whose original home is Rosscullen, should be the one leading his community into the opportunities of the new century, but he is too indecisive, too cynical, and too skeptical about the abilities of his fellow Irish to commit himself, assume the leadership that is needed, and marry the Irish girl, Nora, who loves him and has been waiting for him. Therefore the ever-optimistic Englishman and his countrymen will inherit by default and grow wealthy by capitalist exploitation.

The spokesperson for socialism who has a program for a utopian state is the unfrocked Catholic priest, Peter Keegan. But he is an eccentric visionary who sometimes talks to grasshoppers. He is a St. Francis, but without the political authority to alter the inevitable results of the English affection for and obsession with John Bull's other island.

Some of Shaw's funniest character creations and most challenging, thought-provoking dialogue grace this great Irishman's humorous "plague o' both your houses!" Today Shaw's views on Home Rule are of interest primarily to historians, but his delightfully satiric representations of the conflicting Irish and English characters—and the mixed-message, postcolonial colonialism of a wealthier, ever-patronizing Britain towards its small neighbor and its seemingly quixotic population—are astoundingly relevant still.

In 1905, a year after *John Bull's Other Island* opened in London, King Edward VII ordered a royal command performance; convulsed with laughter, he broke his chair and fell to the floor. In the end the Irish had the last laugh.

Additional Reading

Gordon, David J. *Bernard Shaw and the Comic Sublime.* New York: St. Martin's, 1990.

Shaw, George Bernard. *George Bernard Shaw's Collected Plays with Their Prefaces.* Edited by Dan H. Laurence. New York: Dodd, Mead: 1970–1974.

Smith, Warren Sylvester. *Bishop of Everywhere: Bernard Shaw and the Life Force.* University Park, Pa.: Pennsylvania State Univ. Press, 1982.

John Millington Synge
(1871–1909)

More than any other Irish dramatist, John Millington Synge captured the harsh truths, the painful lives, the soothing, necessary blind faith, the poetry of the oral tradition, and the humor of the poor folk of Ireland's West. Synge was the first truly world-class Irish dramatist of the modern age who worked in the Irish theater, and his comic masterpiece, *The Playboy of the Western World*, the glory of early twentieth-century Irish drama, is the most frequently performed and read Irish play of the early period.

Edmund John Millington Synge was born of Protestant stock in Rathfarnham, County Dublin, to a lawyer and Galway landowner, John Hatch Synge, who died a year after Synge was born, and Katheen Traill Synge, a daughter of an evangelical Ulster Protestant clergyman. Synge, the youngest of five children, grew up and spent much of his life among women—mother, grandmother, and sister. Thus the strong older women in his plays. After early private education, he attended Trinity College, Dublin, and the Royal Irish Academy of Music simultaneously, becoming an Academy orchestra member as a violinist determined on a career as a professional musician. At this phase of his life, he rejected his inherited formal religion to become an individualistic lover of nature, a mystic, and an aesthete.

In pursuit of advanced musical training, Synge journeyed to Germany in 1893, where he suddenly decided on a writer's career and thus moved to Paris, then the center of European culture and literature. On vacations he visited Ireland's west coast and made his first trip out to the Aran Islands. Back in Paris he met Yeats, who advised him to return to Ireland, especially to the Aran Islands, to find his subjects, narratives, and language.

From 1899 to 1902, Synge was a regular and accepted summer visitor on the Islands, listening, observing, and taking notes on the ancient and isolated life of the fisher folk. Synge's first book, *The Aran Islands*, illustrated by Yeats's talented brother, Jack B. Yeats, was published in 1907. Meanwhile, Synge began to write plays for the new Irish National Theatre. Synge's two great one-acters, *In the Shadow of the Glen* (1903) and *Riders to the Sea (1904)* were his brilliant first efforts in a genre completely new to him.

After the opening of the Abbey Theatre in 1904, Synge became one of its directors, and the next year *The Well of the Saints* was first produced there. In 1907, *The Playboy of the Western World* provoked a riot at its Abbey opening, nationalists objecting to its portrayal of the Irish character and others objecting to the mention of a woman's undergarment in public. Synge's last play, *The Tinker's Wedding*, written in 1902 and published in 1908, was not produced by the Abbey in Synge's lifetime because of its anticlerical scenes.

Synge died of Hodgkin's disease on 24 March 1909, before completing his last play, *Deidre of the Sorrows.* His work was already a success in London, and soon the Abbey Company would take it to America for more riots and everlasting fame. The early international recognition of modern Irish drama as a major contributor to world theater and literature rested on the handful of plays Synge left behind. A generation later O'Casey renewed and enhanced that recognition.

Plays

Synge's plays, in spite of comic elements, are often melancholy works. The heroes are sweet-talking men who try to take
the women of their choice from their staid domestic worlds into
the adventure of life. His plays, so full of truth that they hurt,
were always events. And in time they became part of the national
life of Ireland.

In the Shadow of the Glen (1904)

Although Synge first heard the story on Inishmaan in the
Aran Islands, he chose to set his play in a Wicklow glen near his
home, Glenmalure. The story of a jealous old man pretending to
be dead in order to test the fidelity of his young wife, however, is
an ancient one, as is the tale of the eternal triangle of the old husband, the young wife, and a young lover. Both have been used for
tragedy and comedy, and both contribute to Synge's plot. Nora
Burke's old husband, Dan, is distasteful to her. For her, the marriage was based on her desire to have some security in her life.
Dan, for his part, in the pattern of Irish marriages of the past,
"with a bit of a farm with cows on it, and sheep on the back hills,"
had waited until late in life to marry a young, strong, and desir-
able woman.

Tricked into believing that her husband is dead, Nora and her
young lover, Michael Dara, plan to take his money and marry, although she has some reservations about life with Michael being a
repeat of life with old Dan. Michael is concerned primarily with
the money. Then Dan "rises from the dead" and orders Nora out
of his house.

The cowardly, parsimonious Michael will not go out into the
world with the penniless woman. Instead, she departs with a
tramp, a symbol of freedom, who promises her song, sun, and a
good companion in bed. The husband and the lover, instead of

falling to blows, are content in the end to drink to each other's health in whiskey, the water of life. The play is a tragicomedy, much more Irish than Greek, for in the end the vital woman seems superfluous as the contending men are happy and sociable in their friendship and their drink.

Riders to the Sea (1904)

The only play of Synge's set in the Aran Isles, *Riders to the Sea* is the playwright's darkest, most tragic drama. The presence of irrevocable fate is so strong in the play—and it so engrossed Synge's creative sensibilities—that for the first and only time in his dramas language recedes and plot takes center stage.

Central to the drama is the character of Maurya, one of the first archetypal, all-suffering, all-sacrificing Irish mothers in modern Irish drama. She has given her husband and one son to the sea, and now she must watch helplessly as yet another son, Bartley, her last, wills himself to ride the horses to the sea and the eternity that the sea symbolizes. Maurya must tell the story, just as she must do her duty to provide clothing for the living and coffins for the dead and then to keen. Men, cut off in their prime, continually enter the cemetery of the sea, as Maurya reminds us: "There does be a power of young men floating round in the sea."

Bartley, almost perversely, dies not as a fisherman but from a riding accident at the shore, as a wild young man determined to take his animals to the horse fair on the mainland. But the fateful sea will claim its catch as it can. The tragedy of *Riders to the Sea* is the most ancient of all, the greatest grief: the death of the young before the old.

The Well of the Saints (1905)

Synge's knowledge of French literature served him well: *The Well of the Saints* is based in part on a French morality play of the fifteenth century. His two blind, indigent protagonists, Martin and Mary Doul, surely inspired Beckett's creation of more than one beggarly pair (as in *Endgame* and *Waiting for Godot*). In morality plays, names of characters are significant and help in characterization. *Doul* is Irish for blind, and this blind couple are a happy couple despite their affliction. They rant, rave, and abuse each other, but they live contentedly in their own world, and it is a rich, variegated, and beautiful one because it exists in their colorful imaginations. They each believe, for example, that the other is very attractive, while in fact they are far from it.

The saint at the well miraculously restores their sight. Although at first they are delighted, they soon come to realize each other's and then their own ugliness—and how unpleasant looking and acting the world and the sighted are. They no longer have a great deal to say to each other. Their worlds are now individually different, and each one seems too large.

Now they must toil for a living, pitifully paid as road workers. They separate for a while, but as their sight dims again, they rediscover each other and reunite in their happy relationship. Realizing that they have been misused by the controlling holy man, they spurn the saint, his asceticism, and his miracles. Although the blind couple are driven out on to the road by the villagers, a higher place is clearly waiting for them. It is the palace of self-knowledge, reason, sensuality, and confidence, as evidenced by Mary's curtain line: "The Lord protect us from the Saints of God."

The Playboy of the Western World (1907)

Synge succeeded in his stated goal for *The Playboy of the Western World*, to write in "English that is perfectly Irish in essence." The language, the broad characterizations, the humor, the precise structure, and the satire of the play are so excellent that without doubt the play is not only a masterpiece but the greatest single play ever to have been written in Ireland.

The setting of *The Playboy* is a country public house in Mayo. Although its publican is Michael Flaherty, it is his daughter Pegeen who does most of the work and runs the establishment. She is betrothed to Shawn Keogh, an unattractive, cowardly, priest-ridden cousin, for whom neither she nor the audience has much respect.

A pitiful fugitive, Christy Mahon, comes into the house, and when he announces that he has murdered his father, a farmer like himself, the unprepossessing young man becomes an instant hero to Pegeen and the community. Even an older woman, the wily Widow Quin, sets her cap for him. But Christy cares for Pegeen, and she is in love with the young "hero," who conjectures, "Wasn't I the foolish fellow not to kill my father in the years gone by?"

After preening himself and milking the situation, the now cocky Christy finds his story finally unraveling when his father appears, head slightly dented, but very much alive. Christy, who actually believed he had killed his father, now has lost face, and so he "kills" him again. But this time the community is aghast; as Pegeen says, "there's a great gap between a gallous story and a dirty deed," and she even burns him to break his hold on a table. But Old Mahon is still not "killed." He reappears, this time full of admiration for his son because, in confronting his father, Christy has proved his manhood.

Christy now disdains Pegeen and the community and marches off with his father following respectfully. The young hero has, in the tradition of comedy, overcome the impediment of older generational power. But poor Pegeen utters the lament of many a young Irish woman: "Oh, my grief, I've lost him surely. I've lost the only playboy of the Western World."

The Playboy of the Western World is the finest Irish comedy just as *The Importance of Being Earnest* is the finest English comedy. Of course, they were both written by Irishmen. Both plays are ultimately about language: the profound incongruity between the poetry and wit of a delightfully crafted story and the realities of life that words distort or incompletely signify.

The Tinker's Wedding (written 1902, significantly revised for publication in 1908)

Because of its anticlerical thrust and a scene in which a grasping parish priest is gagged and tied up for his willingness to let a couple go without the sacrament of marriage unless they meet his material demands, the Abbey did not put on *The Tinker's Wedding* until 1971. The Rabelaisian comedy pits Michael Byrne, a crafty tinker—that is, a person of the roads who lives like a gypsy but is not actually one—against a priest who wants to extract as much money and goods for his services as he can. The tinker's companion, Sarah Casey, craves middle-class respectability, and thus wishes to be married. Michael reluctantly agrees to have his relationship with his woman sanctified by marriage, because, like a bourgeois, he has patriarchal economic reasons for tying up his woman as wife: "If I didn't marry her, she'd be off walking to Jaunting Jim maybe at the fall of night, and . . . there isn't the like of her for getting money and selling songs to the men."

He wants to keep possession of her sexual favors and her earning ability. The priest is reluctantly willing to marry the couple for the seemingly bargain price of half a sovereign, but he also wants a can (drinking vessel) that the tinker (traditionally a pot mender and tinsmith) is making. Michael tries to trick the priest out of the can, but the priest then refuses to marry the couple and orders them off. The tinkers tie him, gag him with the sack that had held the can, and then, in an ending like a Ben Jonson comedy, the couple run for their lives. Of course, Michael and Sarah will continue to live in sin, although they pledge their troth to each other in a "Tinker's Wedding."

The play feels and sounds like a medieval folk play. Farce provides much of the humor, and rich characterization makes *The Tinker's Wedding* a play that has grown in popularity as an alternative to the more often produced *Playboy* and *The Well of the Saints*.

Deidre of the Sorrows (1910)

Completed by Yeats and Lady Gregory, the tragedy *Deidre of the Sorrows* was premiered by the Abbey in the year after Synge's death. The signature Synge language enriches the play, and it is certainly warmer and more feeling than Yeats's *Deidre*, but in the end the story remains more fitted for the romantic poem of earlier versions than a workable drama.

The play is passionate. Deidre's and Naisi's love is erotic and ecstatic. The Celtic past is presented in soft-focus nostalgia. Yet the plot line is timeless and international: the dark and deadly triangle of an old man, his young bride, and her young lover. Conchubor, the cuckolded king, is like a darker Arthur; his jealousy-inspired treachery in luring the heroine, the hero, and his two brothers back to Ireland from Scotland—resulting in the deaths of the three men and the suicide of Deidre—is terrible but humanly understandable.

Young love cut off is paradoxically both mortal and immortal. But the consequences of adultery and revenge are catastrophic: a palace in flames and a kingdom on the verge of destruction. Synge gives the persuasive Deidre, who almost convinces her husband to spare her lover, a great last speech, one that echoes that of Shakespeare's Cleopatra. It includes lines that are as true for Synge as for any mythic hero or heroine: "I have put away sorrow like a shoe that is worn out and muddy, for it is I have had a life that will be envied by great companies."

Additional Reading

Greene, David H., and Edward M. Stephens. *J. M. Synge 1871–1909*. New York: Macmillan, 1959.

Grene, Nicholas. *Synge: A Critical Study of the Plays*. London: Macmillan, 1975.

Kiberd, Decan. *Synge and the Irish Language*. London: Macmillan, 1979.

King, Mary C. *The Drama of J. M. Synge*. Syracuse, N.Y.: Syracuse Univ. Press, 1985.

Synge, John Millington. *J. M. Synge: Complete Works*. London: Oxford Univ. Press, 1968.

10

Other Early Modern Dramatists

Of course, other playwrights besides Lady Gregory, Yeats, and Synge contributed to the growth, development, and success of the Irish drama before O'Casey. Outstanding among these dramatists were Padraic Colum, T. C. Murray, George Fitzmaurice, Lennox Robinson, and George Shiels. Of these early writers, Padraic Colum was the one who seemed most destined for greatness and perhaps literary immortality.

Padraic Colum (1881–1972)

Padraic Colum liked to say that of all the Irish playwrights of his time, he was the only one who was Roman Catholic and peasant born. He also liked to say that he was born in the workhouse of Longford, which was technically true, but his father was master there. Colum's mother was the daughter of a gardener. With a minimum of education, Colum followed his father to Sandycove, County Dublin, to work as a railway clerk. Beginning to write poems and one-act plays, he came to the attention of Arthur Griffith, editor of *The United Irishman* and later first president of the Irish Free State. Colum linked up with the Abbey as both playwright and actor. The three full-length plays he wrote between 1903 and 1910—*Broken Soil* (1903), revised and retitled *The Fiddler's House* for the 1907 revival; *The Land* (1905), and *Thomas Muskerry (1910)*—established him briefly as the Abbey's most popular playwright.

The brash young writer, who also had great initial success as a lyric poet with his first collection of poems, *The Wild Earth* (1907), quarreled with Yeats and the Abbey company, and despite the attempt of Lady Gregory to effect a reconciliation, he quit the company. In 1914 he left for America with his wife, Mary Colum, who in New York became one of America's leading critics of the early twentieth century. Colum had no success as a playwright in New York, try as he would, but continued to publish well-received and still revered volumes of poetry, folklore, and children's books, until his death in Connecticut just before his ninety-first birthday. One of his most popular nondramatic books is *Our Friend James Joyce* (1958), which he coauthored with his wife.

The Fiddler's House (first titled *Broken Soil,* 1903, revised and revived, 1907)

Conn Hourican is a middle-aged peasant farmer who has to choose between the romantic life of an itinerant musician and his obligation to his children and the land. The allegorical play pits Hourican, the freedom-loving artist, against James Moynihan, the grasping son of a miserly father. Conn chooses the road, and his loving daughter Maire goes with him; but her lover, Brian, woos her back. The play's strength is its authentic depiction of peasant characters.

The Land (1905)

Produced at the Abbey on 9 June 1905, just six months after the theater opened, *The Land* was the new theater's first popular success—to some extent because it was about the fairly recently concluded "land war" and the passage of the Land Purchase Act, which allowed peasant farmers for the first time the opportunity to purchase and own the land on which they and their families had worked for centuries.

Two elderly farmers, Murtagh Cosgar and Martin Douras, try to keep their children on the land by arranging two marriages. In the end, however, the bright couple leave to emigrate to America, and the good-hearted but dull couple remain to inherit the land. Colum is saying that for many land ownership came too late and the best of the young were and are leaving. The lamented emigration of talented youth has remained a vital theme in Irish drama to the present.

Thomas Muskerry (1910)

Based on Colum's recollection of life in the Longford workhouse his father administered, *Thomas Muskerry* is his only pure tragedy. It resembles *King Lear* in its portrayal of a workhouse master who in his old age is treated cruelly by his daughter, who in turn is mistreated by her daughter. Colum is showing how hardheartedness is passed on from generation to generation as well as how frail and fleeting human dignity is.

Additional Reading

Colum, Padraic. *Selected Plays*. Edited by Sanford Sternlicht. Syracuse, N.Y.: Syracuse Univ. Press, 1986.
————. *Three Plays*. Dublin: Maunsel, 1917.
Sternlicht, Sanford. *Padraic Colum*. Boston: Twayne, 1985.

T. C. Murray (1873–1959)

Thomas Cornelius Murray was born in Macroom, County Cork. He trained as a primary school teacher at St. Patrick's Teachers' Training College in Drumcondra, and education remained his primary work until he retired from teaching in 1932.

T. C. Murray was a playwright who invested almost his entire stock in dramatic realism; his best plays offer a grim and often tragic portrait of Irish peasant life. He also strove to show the religion of the peasant, Irish Catholicism, in a kinder light than other early modern Irish dramatists. *Maurice Hart* (1912) and *Autumn Fire* (1924) today are considered his finest dramas.

Maurice Harte (1912)

Combining Ibsen-like social drama and the peasant scene, much in the manner of Padraic Colum's *Thomas Muskerry* (1910), *Maurice Harte* is the story of devoted parents who have sacrificed almost everything to educate a son for the priesthood only to find that the son has lost his vocation for the life of a priest. The father and mother, Michael and Ellen Harte, entreat their son, Maurice, to return to the priesthood for their sakes. Moved by his mother's pleas, Michael miserably decides to go back. In the end, however, he has a nervous breakdown from the stress, and his parents, especially his mother, are filled with guilt. The convincing dialogue and the powerful characterization are the primary strengths of this play of religious struggle.

Autumn Fire (1924)

An elderly widower, Owen Keegan, proud of his good health and physical prowess, marries a woman thirty years his junior. The community disapproves. His daughter, Ellen, is angered, and his son, Michael, evidences his own interest in the bride, Nance. Owen soon suffers a stroke, and Michael grows closer to Nance, so Ellen makes her father jealous. Though Michael must leave home, and the invalid father cannot believe in his wife's innocence, the blighted marriage goes on. The archetypal story is as current today as it was in the Athens of Euripides or in early twentieth-century Ireland.

Additional Reading

Connolly, Terrence L. "T. C. Murray, the Quiet Man." *Catholic World* 190 (Mar., 1960), 364–69.

Murray, T. C. *Autumn Fire*. London: Allen and Unwin, 1928.

————. *Maurice Harte*. Dublin: Maunsel, 1912.

George Fitzmaurice (1877–1963)

Born the son of a Protestant minister who had crossed the line to marry a Roman Catholic girl, George Fitzmaurice grew up between cultures and eventually seemed to fall in the crack. He spent most of his youth with his mother's peasant Catholic family but was gentry by birth because his paternal relatives were of the Ascendancy.

Fitzmaurice's life was to a large extent that of a recluse. He moved to Dublin in 1901, and his first play at the Abbey was *The Country Dressmaker*, presented in 1907. The comedy remained a favorite play for Abbey audiences for some forty years. He served in the British Army in World War I and became a civil servant to earn his living, working for the Department of Agriculture until retirement. He died in an impecunious state.

George Fitzmaurice followed close on the heels of Synge and Colum with his peasant plays. The typical locale is a peasant cottage. Although Fitzmaurice's themes, like Colum's, are marriage, emigration, and the lust for land, he differs from Colum in his use of the fantastical and the whimsical. Almost all of his seventeen plays are set in the world of his childhood, the northern region of County Kerry, and he attempts to replicate the local dialect in his dramas.

The Pie-Dish (1908)

In *The Pie-Dish*, a one-act fantasy, Fitzmaurice employs his characteristic technique of mixing realistic situations with the fantastical and supernatural. The story is of a dying old man, Leum Donoghue, who desperately fears that he will not be able to complete an ornamental dish on which he has been working for twenty years. To buy more time, he offers his soul to the devil. The tricky devil accepts. But when Donoghue finishes the dish, it falls from his hands and shatters just as he drops dead. It's the old Faustian bargain, of course, but the audience loved its irony and its Irish setting.

The Magic Glasses (1913)

The one-act play *The Magic Glasses* is set in Padden and Maineen Shanahan's kitchen. Jaymony Shanahan, their thirty-eight-year-old son, spends his time in a loft looking through nine lenses purchased from a fairy. Through them he sees a better world, a fantastic place. A conflict results because his desire to merge with his fantasy world causes him to behave strangely, alarming his family.

Believing Jaymony mad, they call in a charlatan miracle worker, Mr. Quille, to cure him. Quille blasphemously "exorcises" Jaymony, prescribes a ridiculous regimen, and departs, but the devil seems to have possessed the family, for the loft collapses, with Jaymony falling to his death, and the other inhabitants rush out of the house, screaming in terror. A madness that should have been only humorous and harmless has ended in death and catastrophe; the audience, like witnesses to a morality play in the Middle Ages, is stunned by the powerful, frightening, melodramatic denouement.

Additional Reading

Fitzmaurice, George. *The Plays of George Fitzmaurice.* 3 vols. Dublin: Dolmen, 1967, 1969, 1970.

Gelderman, Carol W. *George Fitzmaurice.* Boston: Twayne, 1979.

McGuinness, Arthur E. *George Fitzmaurice.* Lewisburg, Pa., Bucknell Univ. Press, 1975.

Lennox Robinson (1886–1958)

Best known as the Abbey manager and then director, Lennox Robinson was also a playwright, novelist, essayist, and theater historian, as well as the author of a two-volume autobiography. His well-made plays featured middle-class, small-town Irish life.

Esme Stuart Lennox Robinson, the son of a Protestant clergyman, was born in Douglas, County Cork, and educated at Bandon Grammar School. He saw the Abbey Company performing on tour in Cork in 1907 and fell in love with the theater. Off and on and in various posts, Robinson served the Abbey as an administrator from 1909 to his death in 1958. His first Abbey play was *The Clancy Name* (1908). His best-known plays are the comedy *The Whiteheaded Boy* (1916) and the Chekhovian drama *The Big House* (1926). Much honored at the end of his life, Robinson is buried in St. Patrick's Cathedral, Dublin.

The Whiteheaded Boy (1916)

The working-class comedy *The Whiteheaded Boy* depicts how some younger sons wind up in no-win situations. The older siblings of Denis Georghegan scrimp and save and sacrifice futures to send him to a university in order for him to receive a medical degree. But Denis does not want to be a doctor, nor does he have a particular aptitude for medicine. The siblings have not sacrificed cheerfully but somewhat grumpily, and, when Denis leaves to become a laborer, one would expect they would be glad to no longer have the expense. However, they now join forces to prevent such a disgrace to the family. The story and its ironies are engaging.

The Big House (1926)

Given the current nostalgia for the Irish country mansion and its Ascendancy inhabitants and the popularity of Brian Friel's play about an Irish Big House, *The Aristocrats* (1979), there should be a revival of *The Big House* soon. When Robinson wrote the play, it seemed that none of the great houses would survive; nearly two hundred of them had been destroyed between 1921 and 1923, the period of the last months of the Anglo-Irish War and the Post-Treaty Irish Civil War. *The Big House* presents the dilemma of a well-meaning, socially responsible Ascendancy landlord family, the Alcocks, as they are trapped in a struggle based on both political and class based differences. *The Big House* is Ballydonal House in County Cork, where the Alcock family learns on Armistice Day, 11 November 1918, that the second and last son has, like his brother before, been killed in action in France. Subsequently the house, very much a character in the play, is threatened with destruction by Irish guerrillas during the Anglo-Irish War—as retaliation when the Black and Tans, British rampaging auxiliary police, are randomly killing—but it is spared because of the loyalty and respect of the village people. But later in the Civil War, Ballydonal is burned by republicans, and the family breaks up. The father and mother retire to England, but the sensitive daughter Kate realizes that regardless of class or religion she is Irish, not English. Thus she plans to rebuild, continuing to make her lonely life in the country of her birth as it is being reborn as an independent state.

As in Chekhov's *The Cherry Orchard*, a family is caught up in forces far beyond its control, but in this play, unlike Chekhov's, a tradition and an estate rebuilt will live on and contribute to the new era. *The Big House* is a moving play of historical significance and a fine piece of theater. Kate Alcock is one of the best-drawn women in the early modern Irish school of realism.

Additional Reading

Murray, Christopher, ed. *Selected Plays of Lennox Robinson*. Washington, D.C.: Catholic University of America Press, 1982.

O'Neill, Michael J. *Lennox Robinson*. New York: Twayne, 1964.

George Shiels (1886–1949)

Born in Ballymoney, County Antrim, George Shiels emigrated to Canada in 1906 but returned to Antrim seven years later after suffering crippling injuries in a train accident. Shiels took up writing without any formal instruction in the craft. He was, like Fitzmaurice, quiet and reclusive; although he was a very popular dramatist, he hardly ever left his home in Carnlough even to see a play of his performed.

George Shiels gave Ireland snapshots of itself in the between-the-wars period, in realistic, gently satirical comedies and dramas based on the new country's need for equal justice and for law and order. His play-writing career began with two one-act plays performed at the Ulster Literary Theatre in Belfast: *Under the Moss* (1918) and *Felix Reid and Bob* (1919). His first plays for the Abbey, *Bedmates* and *Insurance Money*, both also one-act plays, were produced in 1921. His first major successes were *Paul Twyning* (1922) and *Professor Tim* (1925). With these works Shiels established his own brand of rural Ulster kitchen comedy, complete with cleverly subdued social commentary. *The Passing Day* (1936) is Shiels's strongest, most satirical, and bitterest play. In 1940, *The Rugged Path* broke Abbey Theatre records, playing to 25,000 people in eight weeks. In the period after O'Casey, Shiels was the mainstay of the Abbey Theatre. All in all, he wrote twenty-three plays, including full-length ones as well as one-acters. *Professor Tim* was made into a Hollywood film.

Paul Twyning (1922)

The title character is an itinerant laborer who enjoys mischief making. A skillful liar who convinces people of his truthfulness, he sets about to disrupt a family, turning members against each other. James Deegan, a Magistrate of the Crown, a person new to money and middle-class status, is his chief victim. Love and lovers play a part in the comedy. Paul turns suitors against each other; but, in the convention of romantic comedy, the right men win the predestined brides, and even Paul winds up with a lover.

The Passing Day (1936)

Set in six scenes that take place in one day, *The Passing Day* is the story of three mean characters living in a small town filled with an unsavory population. John Fibbs, a wealthy merchant and town leader, is a sly, miserly, hard old man. His wife Sarah is a resentful puritan. His nephew Peter, adopted as their only child, pretends, like Edmund in *King Lear*, to be an obedient son, but he really would like to murder his hated uncle. (Peter himself is incapable of loving anyone, even his devoted girlfriend.) At the beginning of the play Fibbs is on his deathbed in the hospital. In the course of the play, all who try to extract money or advantage from Fibbs are exposed: wife, doctor, lawyer, nephew, acquaintances. *Passing Day* is much like Ben Jonson's *Volpone*—as biting, if not as funny.

Additional Reading

Kennedy, David. "George Shiels: A Playwright at Work." *Threshold* 25 (summer 1974), 50–78.

Shiels, George. *"The Passing Day"* and *"The Jailbird."* London: Macmillan, 1937.

————. *Three Plays: "Professor Tim," "Paul Twynning," "The New Gossoon."* London: Macmillan, 1945.

11
•••

Sean O'Casey
(1880–1964)

After Synge the next truly world-renowned dramatist to arise from the Irish theater was Sean O'Casey. His three tragicomedies, *The Shadow of a Gunman* (1923), *Juno and the Paycock* (1924), and *The Plough and the Stars* (1926), are all centered on the then-recent events of the War of Independence and the Civil War and set in the Dublin slums he knew so well. They turned the Irish theater for a while towards bitter social criticism with O'Casey's dark thesis that the acclaimed and glorified birth of a nation was accompanied by the pathetic suffering, powerlessness, and tragedy of the unknown and little-regarded common people swept up and drowned in the raging, mindless torrent of history.

O'Casey was a self-taught playwright. He came to his art by seeing some plays in Dublin, but mostly by reading Ibsen and Strindberg, Shakespeare and the other Elizabethans. He also read the plays of the most popular Irish dramatist of the nineteenth century, Dion Boucicault, from whom he learned much about dramatic structure.

O'Casey is the playwright of the disintegrating community and of the fragile family that in the end has only love (and even that can't be counted on). O'Casey's ear for the dialect of the Dublin tenements is very sharp. He had heard enough of it. Like

Synge, he shaped and lyricized dialogue, adding dignity to the utterances of the poor.

After the Dublin trilogy O'Casey, having written out of his system much of his cynicism and skepticism towards Irish government, patriotism, religion, and politics, became more and more an experimental dramatist. But *The Shadow of a Gunman, Juno and the Paycock,* and *The Plough and the Stars* stand as monuments that rose unexpectedly in the shadow of the Abbey—and out of the pain of a compassionate person who shared with many the disillusion with life and society's institutions in the aftermath of the heady achievement of independence that, alas, did not lead to promised peace or work or food.

He was born John Casey, the youngest of thirteen children in a lower-middle-class Dorset Street, Dublin, Protestant family that sank to working-class status after the death of the father when O'Casey was three. Crowded Dublin was an unhealthy place for children in the late nineteenth century, and eight of O'Casey's siblings died in childhood. He himself was sickly and troubled with lifelong vision problems (perhaps caused by malnutrition) that prevented him from obtaining more than a cursory elementary education. He was a teenager before he learned to read.

O'Casey found employment as a laborer. At night he pursued his religious and political interests: his local church; the Orange Lodge for Protestant men; the Gaelic League, where he studied Irish; the Irish Republican Brotherhood; and the Irish Citizen Army, the political and militant arm of the Irish Transport and General Workers' Union. But one by one, his organizations disappointed him, and, disgruntled, he shed them all. He began writing journalism, history, poetry, and even greeting-card verses for a Dublin publisher. Eventually he came to dramatic writing after realizing in his forties that he could use his lifetime of observing Dublin tenement life to provide authentic dialogue.

In 1923, O'Casey offered a two-act play, *On the Run,* to the

Abbey. Lady Gregory was enthusiastic. It was put on at the season's end as *The Shadow of a Gunman*. Tenement life in Dublin, which other writers had treated with little success, had its first fully effective dramatic portrayal with O'Casey. *Juno and the Paycock* and *The Plough and the Stars* quickly followed. The latter, however, was greeted with hostility by the audience and brought riots once more in and about the Abbey. An Irish writer seemed to be ridiculing Irish patriotism, nationalism, and the Irish character. Yeats's reaction was a speech to the audience in which, alluding to the riots over *The Playboy of the Western World*, he said, "You have disgraced yourselves again!"

Hurt, O'Casey took the play to London, where he had received the Hawthornden Prize for *Juno and the Paycock*. In London he married an Irish actress, Eileen Carey, who performed in West End productions of his plays. O'Casey's next play, experimental and expensive to mount, was a drama on World War I, *The Silver Tassie*, written in 1928. To his surprise and chagrin, it was rejected by the Abbey. Yeats was ungracious and ungenerous this time; he didn't like modernist dramas and World War I subjects. The Abbey eventually put on the play in 1936. But the angry O'Casey exiled himself from Ireland forever.

O'Casey wrote many more plays after *The Silver Tassie*,—fantasies, expressionist dramas, moralities—but he never again penned a play that was a popular and critical success. Several of his later plays and his autobiographies reflect his commitment to socialism and communism. His bad temper, sharp tongue, tactlessness, and critical and fractious nature alienated many colleagues in the theatrical world.

If any playwright learned from the early O'Casey, it was his fellow Dubliner Brendan Behan, who appreciated O'Casey's work with dialect, his efforts to recognize the existence of the urban poor, and his desire to portray their lives with dignity. Behan also understood and employed the O'Casey technique of blending humor, pathos, and tragedy.

Today, of the playwrights who came into prominence in the tenure of Lady Gregory and Yeats at the Abbey, O'Casey is the most frequently performed in Ireland and probably on the world stage.

Plays

Although the central themes of O'Casey's great plays, the Dublin trilogy, are always serious, even tragic, they contain superb dialogue, wonderfully humorous characterizations, and some of the most hilariously comic scenes in modern drama. O'Casey shows his great love for and understanding of humanity, for his tenement people are all the common people of this sad, frightened, and frightening world.

The Shadow of a Gunman (1922)

Set in a Dublin tenement room during the 1920 conflict between Irish guerrillas and the Black and Tan, *The Shadow of a Gunman* is the story of a working-class poet, Donal Davoren, who shares the room with a peddler named Seamas Shields. The other inhabitants of the house believe Donal is a rebel gunman hiding out, and, basking in unearned respect and prestige; he does not correct their assumptions. Like many if not most of the author's men, the poet and the pedlar are lazy cowards, and their lives are essentially aimless; it is the women of the plays who have courage and energy. To save Donal, Minnie Powell, a young worker in the tenement, removes bombs left in the room by a rebel, and she is shot by the Black and Tans. The men live on to stew in their shame and ignominy.

The Shadow of a Gunman indicates the beginnings of O'Casey's superb characterizations and his comic gifts. Donal and Seamas, who wait and cringe instead of acting, are among the forerunners of Vladimir and Estragon in *Waiting for Godot*. Written when the

War of Independence had just concluded, the play evidences O'-Casey's commitment to truth and his personal political courage.

Juno and the Paycock (1924)

O'Casey's masterpiece, *Juno and the Paycock*, is set contemporaneously in a Dublin slum flat inhabited by the Boyle family. "Captain" Jack Boyle is the "paycock," who detests work, and who lies, brags, and prefers drinking to all other activities. His sidekick is the parasitic Joxer Daly. They are a team, like a harmful Laurel and Hardy, and they have their theater ancestry in the Miles Gloriosus and the Wily Slave of the Roman comedy of Plautus.

Jack's wife, Juno, is a magnificent women, a rock on whom all the members of a collapsing family cling. She is compassionate and courageous. Her lot is sad, even tragic, but she knows what is right and who is worth saving.

Juno and the Paycock is a play of human waste that is presented as comic as well as tragic. In it O'Casey portrays human greatness in the face of great grief, suffering, and hopelessness. Juno and Jack Boyle have two grown children—hard-luck children. Johnny has been wounded as a guerrilla in the War for Independence, but after the peace treaty he joined the IRA rebels fighting the new Irish government. He is crippled, in pain, and now frightened because he has betrayed the rebels. They come for the traitor, and he is executed.

Mary drops her Irish lover for an Englishman who gets her pregnant and then deserts her. Meanwhile, Jack has been led to believe he has an inheritance coming from the estate of a deceased cousin, and he spends the money before he has it in hand, only to learn that the Englishman's incompetence in drawing up his cousin's will has invalidated the inheritance. Boyle now has creditors breathing down his neck and reclaiming his foolish purchases.

Mary is reviled by her father, and her Irish lover, eager to take her back until he learns she is pregnant, will not stand by her. It is Juno who comforts and supports her daughter. And when the two women leave to view Johnny's body, Jack and Joxer remain behind in drunken reverie. Their comic banter is one of the great pleasures of the play, although they contribute to "the terrible state o' chassis" in their society. Masculine vanity, drinking, and foolishness are the curses on Irish womanhood, implies O'Casey. The family is destroyed, but one believes that Juno and Mary endure and survive, for it is matriarchy that sustains and preserves the race. Unlike the men, Juno is not political. She has no ideology. She is a pragmatic, compassionate human being. She is well named: Juno, a goddess.

The Plough and the Stars (1926)

Like the other plays in the Dublin trilogy, *The Plough and the Stars* is the story of ordinary people caught up in political events that are far beyond their possible control. The title comes from the symbols on the flag of the Irish Transport and General Workers' Union, of which O'Casey was a member. The flag was one of those present at the Easter Rising, as it was also used by the Irish Citizen Army. The title also reflected O'Casey's worker background and identification as well as his lifelong socialism. The play is drawn on a larger scale than the preceding pieces in the Dublin trilogy. Unlike them, it has several settings: two rooms in a tenement flat, the street, and a pub. Also, in order of historical events it precedes them; *The Plough and the Stars* takes place in the months just before the 1916 Easter Rising, which at the time of the writing of the play had not only been recognized as a great turning point in Irish history, but had also taken on mythical proportions as a pageant of patriotism. O'Casey attempts to deflate the heroics by showing that the real heroes, the people of greater courage, are those whose instinctive sympathy and compassion cause them to act kindly, generously, and unselfishly.

Zola-like, O'Casey presents a house full of distinct, interesting, well-drawn, and sometimes comic characters in a play more tragedy than comedy. The young couple Nora and Jack Clitheroe are expecting a child. He is a commandant in the Citizen Army that will fight the British. She attempts to dissuade him from accepting the post but fails because he places honor and patriotism over family. Of course, he is killed, and Nora loses the baby and her mind. Other characters are more memorable, especially the ever-talking Fluther Good, another Joxer Daly kind of character, and the alcoholic Protestant evangelist Bessie Burgess, who dies heroically when she is cut down by a stray bullet while shielding Nora.

Nationalism and nationalist organizations are satirized by rowdy scenes in the pub, looting during the Rising, and the scalding indictment of nationalism by the prostitute Rosie Redmond. In the end, while most of the inhabitants of the slum are cowering in a room, the surviving rebels are led away to prison, accompanied by two British soldiers who sing, ironically enough, "Keep the Home Fires Burning."

In proportions, almost a pageant, *The Plough and the Stars* has great theatrical impact. Its antiheroic stance catches perfectly the mood of most Western nations in the 1920s as their populations refuted the war fever and mindless chauvinism that led Europe to self-destruct in 1914–1918. O'Casey embraced this antiwar disposition and applied it to the heroics of Easter 1916, which, in his view, led to the wasted blood of the War of Independence and the very dirty Irish Civil War.

The Silver Tassie (1929)

In keeping with his antiwar, antinationalism philosophy, one he shared with Shaw, O'Casey wrote the impressionistic *The Silver Tassie*. Rejected by the Abbey, *The Silver Tassie* had its first production in London. The "tassie" is a silver cup awarded to a star football (soccer) player, Harry Heegan, at the height of his career, before the Great War left him a cripple. In the first act O'Casey shows him in his athletic glory. In the third and fourth acts, he is in his wheelchair, paralyzed. At a dance he cannot participate in, he destroys the silver tassie out of frustration and anger.

In O'Casey's previous plays, minor characters enrich the texture, speaking the crisp dialogue that is so characteristic of O'Casey's, and the Abbey's, best work. They often embody the play's humor. In *The Silver Tassie*, however, minor characters are two-dimensional, and their language is equally flat.

The second act, set on the battlefield of northern France, is a powerful piece of expressionist-surrealist theater and a brilliant visual poem of despair, but it does not fit in stylistically with the rest of the drama. Unfortunately, in this play O'Casey let his powerful ideas overcome his dramaturgical instincts and become propaganda. It was and is too "arty" for many, especially after the earthy verisimilitude of the Dublin trilogy.

Additional Reading

Hunt, Hugh. *Sean O'Casey*. Dublin: Gill and Macmillan, 1980.
Krause, David. *Sean O'Casey: The Man and His Work*. Rev. ed. New York: Macmillan, 1975.
O'Casey, Sean. *Collected Plays*. 4 vols. London: Macmillan, 1949–51.
O'Connor, Gary. *Sean O'Casey: A. Life*. New York: Atheneum, 1988.

12
•••

Along with O'Casey

Several other excellent Irish dramatists also contributed to the continuity of the Irish theater during the period dominated by Sean O'Casey. They include Paul Vincent Carroll, Denis Johnston, and M. J. Molloy. Their plays are seldom performed today. But in their time they were popular dramatists on the Irish stage as well as in Britain and America.

Paul Vincent Carroll (1900–1968)

Born at Blackrock, near Dundalk, County Louth, Paul Vincent Carroll was educated at St. Mary's College, Dundalk, and St. Patrick's Training College, Dublin. He emigrated to Scotland when he was twenty-one years old to pursue a career in education. After sixteen years as a Glasgow teacher, he achieved enough writing success to pursue a play-writing career. Carroll's first Abbey play was *Things That Are Caesar's* (1932). His first international success was *Shadow and Substance* (1937). It and *The White Steed* (1939) won major awards in New York.

In 1945, Carroll moved permanently to Britain, where he continued to write plays as well as film and TV scripts. He died in Bromley, Kent. Carroll is perhaps best remembered for his portraits of clergy and the clerical life in his plays Although he was accused of anticlericalism, but his target was not the priesthood itself, but the abuse of power and authority, a perennial theme in modern Irish drama from Synge to the present.

Shadows and Substance (1937)

A paean to humanity's best virtues—goodness, love, and faith—*Shadows and Substance* depicts two proud men and what they represent in conflict: Canon Skerritt and the schoolmaster Dermot O'Flingsley. A good-hearted servant girl, Brigid, who sees a vision of her namesake saint, is advised by O'Flingsley to speak to the canon, but is not treated seriously by the cleric. Later, after she has been accidentally killed in a brawl, both men comprehend that they share some responsibility for her death. In the course of the play, Carroll points out the shortcomings of these hubristic men, who outwardly appear to be pillars of society.

O'Flingsley has published a book that the canon finds subversive, and the cleric wants to use it to get him dismissed. Brigid's death brings them together, making them realize not only that their enmity is dangerous but also that they share moral responsibilities. The play has the subtlety of John Galsworthy's plays, dramas without heroes and with complicated and shifting perspectives.

The White Steed (1939)

In *The White Steed* the kind, likable, fair-minded Canon Matt Lavelle, who is confined to a wheelchair, battles his younger curate, Father Shaughnessy, a puritan sorely afflicted with self-righteousness and narrowness. In the end, a woman once more facilitates reconciliation and redemption. Nora Fintry, a librarian, helps the canon to educate and humanize the curate.

Additional Reading

Carroll, Paul Vincent. *Shadows and Substance*. New York: Random House, 1937.

———. *Three Plays: "The White Steed," "Things That Are Caesar's," and "The Strings, My Lord, Are False."* London: Macmillan, 1944.

Doyle, Paul A. *Paul Vincent Carroll*. Lewisburg, Pa.: Bucknell Univ. Press, 1971.

Denis Johnston (1901–1984)

William Denis Johnston, born in Dublin, was the son of a man who would later sit on the bench of the Supreme Court. After early education in Dublin and Edinburgh, he studied law at Cambridge University and Harvard University. He practiced law for ten years after being called to the bar in Dublin, Belfast, and London.

Johnston also began to write for the theater, in which he had become interested while at Harvard. His first play, *Shadowdance*, was rejected by the Abbey and returned to him with the sentence, "The Old Lady Says 'No'," written on the title page, referring to the fact that Lady Gregory had disapproved. Accordingly, Johnston changed the title to *The Old Lady Says 'No!'*. He knew his revenge would annoy Lady Gregory and the Abbey Theatre, and it did. The play had a successful production in 1929 at the Gate.

Johnston's next play, *The Moon on the Yellow River*, based on the troubles between republicans and the Free State, was accepted by the Abbey and produced there in 1931, but it was not as successful as its predecessor. Johnston had nine plays professionally performed, and he later worked as a producer for the BBC in Belfast, as a wartime journalist, and then as a teacher in American colleges and universities. As a dramatist he always expected his audience to rethink—along with himself—issues and questions of morality and nationalism.

Johnston was married twice, first to Shelah Richards, then to

Betty Chancellor. The novelist Jennifer Johnston is his and Shelah's daughter. He died on 8 August 1984 in Ballybrack, County Dublin.

Johnston was a highly imaginative playwright who moved from experimentalism to realism in his dramatic writing. A man of high intelligence, he was perhaps too cerebral in his work for the theater. A little more emotion might have brought him closer to the achievement of O'Casey in the Dublin trilogy, but Johnston probably didn't want to go quite that way, even when he changed his style to realism.

The Old Lady Says 'No!' (1929)

An experimental play, a director's play of many scenes, *The Old Lady Says "No!"* opens with a playlet concerning the Irish martyr Robert Emmet, leader of the unsuccessful 1803 revolt, who made one of Ireland's greatest speeches at his trial. But Johnston's play is not a historical play extolling Irish nationalism. It is really an expressionist satire on language and how it wears out, unable in the end to serve either the past or the present.

After the opening sequence, in which Emmet is knocked unconscious by the British, the play continues in his mind as he makes an appearance in twentieth-century Dublin looking for his sweetheart Sarah Curran. He plays many roles and, in Brechtian fashion, reminds the audience that they are watching theater, not life. Modern Irish life is presented as squalid, disjointed, and aimless, having been torn loose from the moorings of the past, while the heady nationalism of the 1920s is given a stiff working over, in the manner of O'Casey, that verges on political blasphemy.

Additional Reading

Barnett, Gene A. *Denis Johnston*. Boston: Twayne, 1980.
Johnston, Denis. *The Dramatic Works of Denis Johnston*. 2 vols. Toronto: Macmillan, 1977.

M. J. Molloy (1917–1994)

Born in Milltown, County Galway, Michael Joseph Molloy first trained for the priesthood but was deflected from his vocation by illness. He spent most of his life farming near Milltown. As a writer he embraced the language and the folklore of Ireland's West in a fashion approaching that of Synge. He wrote effectively about the experiences of ordinary Irish people, including the outcasts like peddlers and travelers.

His first play at the Abbey, *The Old Road* (1943), focuses on the depopulation of Ireland's western provinces because of emigration and the lure of the cities. Molloy's finest play is *The King of Friday's Men* (1948). Molloy's drama is distinctively his; there is no mistaking his themes of social disruption and his direct style (much like that of a folk play) for anyone else's. His reclusive life allowed him to concentrate his art on the rural environment in which he lived, the people he spent his life with, and the legends they shared.

The King of Friday's Men (1948)

A nostalgic drama, *The King of Friday's Men*, is part of Molloy's romantic lament for the long-gone Ireland of the preindustrial age. Though set in the eighteenth century, it even recalls heroes of the Celtic past when the hero Bartley Down destroys a contingent of a lord's men with a few bashes from his wide-swinging shillelagh. In this drama western Irish society in Galway and Mayo is still in the grip of feudalism, the hierarchy of lords on top and peasants on bottom. The lord, Caesar French, demands his right to make mistresses of the daughters of his peasants. They choose a betrothed girl, Una Brehony, for the sexual sacrifice, but she is defended by Bartley Dowd.

The droit du seigneur, and the treachery of Caesar French, cause havoc in the country and bring about French's death at the hands of Dowd. The old order is passing, and the rulers of the ancien régime are slow to comprehend the fact. In its epic range and melodramatic energy, the drama reads and plays like a work of Sir Walter Scott.

The Paddy Pedlar (1952)

Molloy's popular one-act play *The Paddy Pedlar* is a macabre comedy that has as its background the beginning of the Famine decade, the 1840s. A thieving, roguish trickster named Ooshla Clancy, who has cheated a young girl, Honor, of her inheritance, tries, with an accomplice, to rob a peddler of what he thinks are stolen riches in his sack. But the peddler is carrying his mother's body to her old home for burial. Shocked at the sight of a corpse instead of the expected loot, Ooshla gives his farm to Honor and her fiancé, while he goes off with the peddler, who will keep him on the straight and narrow with knife pricks, but as a "gentleman" peddler he charges twice what his goods are worth. Black humor is the only way to describe this devilishly clever morality play.

Additional Reading

Hogan, Robert. "Michael Molloy's Dying Ireland." In *After the Irish Renaissance*, 86–98. London: Macmillan, 1968.
Molloy, M. J. *The King of Friday's Men*. Dublin: James Duffy, 1953.

13
•••

Samuel Beckett
(1906–1989)

Samuel Barclay Beckett was born into an affluent Protestant family of mercantile Huguenot origins in Foxrock, one of Dublin's fashionable suburbs south of the city. He was the second son and last child of William Beckett, who worked in the building industry as a successful cost estimator and materials facilitator, and Maria (May) Jones Roe Beckett, who had nursed at the hospital in which William Beckett was briefly a patient. Young Samuel (called Sam) had elementary schooling between the ages of five to nine at the Misses Elsners' Academy near Foxrock. There he began his intense study of French that continued throughout his formal education. From his ninth through his thirteenth year he studied in Dublin as a commuter student at the Earlsfort School. In 1920 he was sent north to study at the Eton-like Portora Royal School in Enniskillen, County Fermanagh, and then he entered Trinity College, majoring in modern languages. He graduated with a B.A. in 1927 and accepted a position teaching French in Belfast at Campbell College, a prestigious public school. Although he later returned to Trinity College as a lecturer in French and subscribed for his M.A. in 1931, Beckett disliked teaching intensely.

In 1929 he went to Paris to work as a lecturer in the Ecole Normale Supérieure. In the French capital, which in the Jazz Age was the avant-garde capital of Western culture, he met and was befriended by James Joyce, who became his mentor. Beckett helped Joyce, whose eyesight was failing, in any way he could—primarily as a reader, although he occasionally took dictation and did research. Unfortunately, Joyce's mentally disturbed daughter, Lucia, fell in love with Beckett, and his rejection of her added to her difficulties. The Joyce family felt Beckett had led Lucia on, though he had not, but cordial relations between the Joyces and the young writer ceased for a time. Nevertheless, James Joyce would always remain a great—perhaps the greatest—linguistic influence on the younger author.

During 1929, Beckett began to publish in magazines, and then his long poem *Whorescope* appeared in book form, followed by his study *Proust*. Returning to Ireland in 1930, Beckett taught French at Trinity, hoping to please his family with a conventional job. But he still hated teaching, and so he walked out on the lectureship and promptly fled back to Paris to escape both Trinity and his pious and difficult mother, with whom he had a love-hate relationship. His infrequent visits to Ireland were always traumatic for the sensitive writer.

In 1932 he returned home again, ill and destitute, to obtain medical treatment and to write. For the first time, he consciously eschewed realism in his creative writing. The next year his beloved and generous father died unexpectedly, but Beckett's *More Pricks than Kicks*, a story collection, was accepted by Chatto and Windus and became his first significant publication in fiction. The chronically depressed young writer, wracked with psychosomatic illnesses, received psychoanalytic treatment in London from 1933 to 1935, where he read extensively in psychology and also heard Carl Jung lecture.

The years up through 1937, when he was writing *Murphy* (1938), his first published novel, were peripatetic ones for Beckett. He moved back and forth, in continual ill health, between London and the family home, Cooldrinagh, in Foxrock. He also had an extended sojourn in Germany to study the language and art, mostly contemporary painting (the painter Jack Yeats was one of his good friends), and to see what was happening to that nation under the repugnant Nazis. After a final break with his smothering mother in 1937, Beckett moved to Paris, the city and its environs that he would make his home for the remainder of his life.

When France was overrun by the Germans in World War II, Beckett committed himself to France, although Eire was neutral, and he courageously joined the French Resistance in 1941. Betrayed along with others in his Resistance unit, he had to flee Paris to hide from the Gestapo in the village of Roussillon (d'Apt) in the Vaucluse, about thirty miles from Avignon, laboring through 1944 as an agricultural worker and helping the Resistance until U.S. troops liberated the village. In 1945 he joined the staff of the Irish Red Cross hospital at St.-Lô. For his services to France he was awarded the Croix de Guerre and the Médaille de la Reconnaissance after the war.

Beckett's major novels were either written in French and translated by himself into English or written in English and translated into French: *Murphy* (1938), *Watt* (written during World War II and published in 1953), *Molloy* (1951), *The Unnamable* (1953), *Malone Dies* (1957), and *How It Is* (1961). All are philosophical works in which Beckett moves from logical positivism to deep, despairing existentialism. It is in Beckett's novels, especially the earlier ones, and in his story collection *More Pricks than Kicks* (1934), that Joyce's influence is most apparent. But unlike Joyce, Beckett was, like Sartre, a secularist, disinterested in myth. He embraced phenomenology. All we get is what we see: namely, this world perceived through our imperfect senses. Nothing transcends the boundaries of human experience.

Waiting for Godot (1954), first written in French as *En Attendant Godot* (1952), is Beckett's masterpiece, a profound statement on the human condition. This minimalist experimental play, which influenced twentieth-century European and American

drama more than any other drama, seemed for a while to have
put an end to realism on the stage and the conventions of the
well-made play: exposition, complication, resolution. It was the
work that led to Beckett's Nobel Prize for Literature in 1969. The
seriocomic ambiguity and puzzling symbolic wordplay of *Godot*,
partly inspired by the dramaturgy of Eugene Ionesco, Jean Genet,
and Arthur Adamov, foreshadow the plays of Tom Stoppard,
Harold Pinter, Edward Albee, and others in the movement once
referred to as the Theatre of the Absurd.

Endgame, a one-act play, appeared in 1958, having first been
written as *Fin de Partie* a year before. *Acte sans Paroles* (1957), a
mime play, became *Act Without Words* (1958). The one-act dramatic monologue *Krapp's Last Tape* (1958), written for the Irish actor Pat Magee, is one of Beckett's most frequently performed
dramas. The ironically titled *Happy Days* appeared in 1961 and
was the last of Beckett's major dramas, although he continued to
write plays with diminishing dialogue and lessening action for
fifteen more years.

Beckett's plays are more theater than drama. They support
performance, pushing it to the foreground. They are spectacular
in the sense that the audience learns almost as much from looking
as from listening. The actor's business in Beckett's dramas is often
slapstick, the effect of silent film comedians like Charley Chaplin
and Buster Keaton on his work. Vladimir and Estragon did not
evolve far from Chaplin's "Little Tramp." The plays, however, are
not mere spectacles: they also became vehicles for polysemous
"readings." Each member of the audience or each reader sees
and/or feels the play, making an individual adoption of it, re-
sponding to the simple but profound words as the archetypal
scenes flood the senses.

After World War II, Beckett, except for occasional trips, spent
the rest of his life in Paris and in a modest country cottage in Ussy,
a village forty miles from the city. Although he had turned down
many honors, Beckett in 1959 accepted an honorary Doctor of Let-

ters from Trinity. In 1961, Beckett married his lover and companion of more than twenty years, Suzanne Deschevaux-Dumesnil, in order to secure an inheritance for her. In 1969 he accepted the Nobel Prize for Literature but did not attend the award ceremony in Stockholm. He and his wife felt the award was a disaster because the notoriety impinged on his writing time and their privacy.

As his fame grew, he became more and more reclusive and secretive. His friends tended more to be artists and theater people than writers. From early manhood he drank copious amounts of Irish whisky and was a heavy smoker.

Up to the last few weeks of his life, Beckett continued to write. After a stay in Le Tiers Temps, a nursing home, Samuel Beckett died of emphysema and Parkinson's disease on 22 December 1989 in the Hôpital Saint-Anne. Suzanne had died on July 17, and he was buried next to her. They had no children.

Waiting for Godot (1954)

It is the great twentieth-century play of inquiring—of skeptical seeking for a meaning for life—of questioning not the existence of God, but the existence of existence. As a minimalist work, *Waiting for Godot* reduces human life to its fundamental pain and its few and small pleasures. Waiting is the being and the end in itself, the only process. And we wait within the prison of our senses. We are alone: that is the essential (or existential) fact of the human condition.

Humankind continues in nihilistic futility, acting irrationally, and not realizing the impossibility of real communication between themselves. The protagonists, two tramps, Vladimir and Estragon, have only their suffering to prove they are alive and only their frail friendship to comfort them. Their world and our world as audience is an almost featureless barren plain. It might as well be the moon except for its one, leafless tree. The tramps are waiting for someone named Godot to rescue them from their misery. But Godot does not come. Instead, a cruel, whip-wielding master, Pozzo, and his demented ex-teacher and slave, Lucky, arrive and stay a short while. Their pause gives Pozzo the opportunity to smoke his pipe, talk about selling Lucky, and give him a kick and then a handkerchief when he sobs. Finally they leave as they came, roped together by Lucky's long tether. At the end of the act, a messenger boy arrives with the announcement, purportedly from Godot, that Godot will come tomorrow.

The second act finds the tree showing five leaves, and the tramps continuing the unending process of waiting. Pozzo and Lucky return and collapse; now Pozzo is blind and Lucky is unable to speak. The tramps help Pozzo up. Lucky will not take advantage of the situation to reverse roles. Pozzo goads him on, and they exit as they had entered. The messenger arrives again and once more states that Godot will come tomorrow. He is questioned about Godot to no avail, and he exits. The tramps try to hang themselves but fail. At nightfall they decide to meet the next day to wait for Godot. Agreeing to leave, they stay. The tragicomedy ends.

It is for the audience to ask and answer its own questions: Where are the tramps and why are they there? What is their relationship? Who is Godot? Does he really exist? Is the messenger telling the truth? What is the meaning of the suddenly blooming tree? What is the significance of the Pozzo-Lucky relationship? Is there any resolution or closure to this stark play, punctuated with black humor? Why can't Vladimir and Estragon go? Why can't they let go?

Waiting for Godot is Samuel Beckett's chief vision of the inner universe, the human mind in the brief interval between the womb and the tomb. It is the end of hope. We wait with Vladimir and Estragon in hopeless hope for the play to end and for life to end. Waiting is the human condition. But if we are waiting for something, someone—Godot or God—we are deceived either by ourselves or by bourgeois society. The existential credo is not the Cartesian "I think, therefore I am" but instead "I suffer, therefore I am."

Endgame (1958)

The one-act play *Endgame* is also about waiting, but as *Waiting for Godot* is about the never-to-be fulfilled promise of a salvational arrival, *Endgame* is about the never-to-be fulfilled promise of a salvational departure. The "endgame" is the last part of a chess game. So the play is the endgame of life as death approaches.

Endgame is set in a bare interior with two small, high-up windows. The room may be the brain and the windows eyes, with nothing to see. Sitting in the middle of the room in a wheelchair is a blind old man, Hamm. He is unable to stand. He wears a scarlet dressing gown that looks like a cardinal's robe, and he has a skull-cap on his head and a blood-soaked handkerchief over his face. His servant, Clov, is standing by the door as the curtain rises. He is unable to sit and can only totter. Hamm and Clov, like Pozzo and Lucky, are bound to each other.

Also on the stage, standing near the wall, are two ash cans, containing Hamm's elderly, legless parents, Nag and Nell, who have lost their legs in a tandem bicycle accident. The characters believe that they are the sole survivors of a great catastrophe. Thus the play is about the end of all human life. Hamm, like Pozzo, is vicious and selfish. Clov would like to leave but cannot. Like Lucky, he is irrevocably tied to a cruel master, and the tension of the drama is the question of Clov's ability to free himself. Hamm has the last food left in the world but cannot feed himself. If Clov leaves, Hamm starves, but so will he. No one can escape the cruel relationships of life: lord and peasant, capitalist and worker, sadist and masochist, wife and husband, friend and enemy, and other binaries.

Near the end of the play, Clov looks out of the window and to his surprise sees a small boy through his telescope. He wonders: "A potential procreator?" But Hamm sums up human despairing indifference: "If he exists he'll die there or he'll come here." Hamm again covers his face, and Clov continues to wait.

With the verbal economy of a modern poem, Beckett has moved humans into their skulls. Action has become meaningless—if it ever had meaning—and the values of Western culture—God, art, family, nation, and love—have no existential reality.

Krapp's Last Tape (1958)

Written for the Irish actor Patrick Magee, *Krapp's Last Tape* is the most popular of Beckett's shorter plays. This one-act monologue is the author's most "Irish play" in that Krapp is clearly an old Irishman listening to his own voice recounting his younger days on his tape recorder and trying to bridge time. Nearly deaf and blind and limping badly, the alcoholic sixty-nine-year-old man listens to a recording he made on his thirty-ninth birthday.

We learn of the death of his mother and the end of his last love affair. He tries to record another story, but his mind wanders off into the realm of vague recollections of his writing career and the mere parody of a love affair. He stops recording and plays "thirty nine" again, allowing the tape to run out into silence as the play concludes. "The rest is silence."

Krapp's Last Tape is not sentimental; it is metaphysical. Krapp is seeking understanding, meaning, knowledge. Beckett chronicles the need of the artist to represent his life through the structure of events. He has looked for his identity in the eyes of his love, and when he asks her, "Let me in," his plea is not merely sexual but a forlorn attempt to establish his existence through the power of their relationship.

Happy Days (1961)

Of course the title is ironic—there are no happy days in Beckett Land. The two-act play, *Happy Days*, presents the most profound female character in Beckett: Winnie, buried like a prehistoric goddess, up to her breasts in the earth.

A "happy day" is the first act, when there is a little less suffering and pain. She is waiting, not for redemption or escape, but for a bell to ring. Like the bell of the mass, or the summoning of the Angelus, or the signal for Pavlov's dog, it will allow her to sleep away the remainder of her life. Next to death, sleep is the preferable condition for humans. Winnie prays, brushes her teeth, spits, and tries without success to communicate with her silent, unseen husband, Willie. She is running out of stores: toothpaste, petroleum jelly, and words.

In the second act Winnie is embedded up to her neck. Things are worse. She no longer prays. She is barely able to understand the meaning of her fragmented phrases and words. As the play nears conclusion, Willie crawls into sight and gropes his way to the pile in which Winnie is embedded, but he can't quite reach her. With his last energy he mutters "Win." Enraptured by this overwhelmingly "joyous" event, Winnie bursts into song with the female part of the waltz duet from *The Merry Widow* as the curtain falls.

Beckett's irony in *Happy Days* is almost unbearable. Human beings are sinking even as they embrace the illusion of love and mutter worn-out words. Winnie and Willie's companionship is absurd, futile, grotesque, and pathetic, yet somehow touching, for what else is there? Perhaps the happy ending to Beckett's last major work is the thought that there is an a priori value after all: human companionship can slightly assuage the pain of human existence, and in the frozen winter of the world you suffer a bit less if someone is with you. So much for the human condition.

Additional Reading

Beckett, Samuel. *Collected Works.* 16 vols. New York: Grove, 1970.
———. *Endgame, A Play in One Act.* New York: Grove, 1958; London: Faber and Faber, 1958.

———. *Happy Days.* New York: Grove, 1961; London: Faber and Faber, 1962.

———. *Krapp's Last Tape.* London: Faber and Faber, 1959; New York: Grove, 1960.

———. *Waiting for Godot.* New York: Grove, 1954; London: Faber and Faber, 1956.

Ben-Zvi, Linda. *Samuel Beckett.* Boston: Twayne: 1986.

Cronin, Anthony. *Samuel Beckett: The Last Modernist,* London: Harper Collins, 1996.

Knowlson, James. *Damned to Fame: The Life of Samuel Beckett.* New York: Simon and Schuster, 1996.

Brendan Behan
(1923–1964)

A beloved writer who himself personified the strengths and weaknesses of many Irishmen, Brendan Francis Behan seemed to win the hearts of Irish people in general and Dubliners in particular. Behan, the son of a house painter, left school (Sisters of Charity in William Street and the Brunswick Street Christian Brothers Seminary) to work in the trade. He was also "schooled" by frequent attendance at the Queen's Theatre and Dublin music halls.

Like his father, a Republican activist who was once imprisoned, Behan joined the IRA. Almost immediately, in December 1939, he was arrested by British Police in Liverpool for possessing explosives and was sentenced as a juvenile to three years in Borstal, a juvenile detention center. Behan was released in December 1941 and returned home to Dublin, only to be arrested again in April for shooting at an Irish detective at a political funeral. This time he was sentenced to fourteen years, serving his time in several prisons, including Mountjoy in Dublin. All in all, Behan spent eight years of his short life behind bars.

While incarcerated, he read voraciously, and he learned Irish from fellow inmates. After general amnesty in 1946 brought about his release, he moved to the West—County Kerry and County Connemara—to attempt to stay out of trouble and to begin a writing career. Returning to Dublin, he was able to make his living with his pen, writing stories and articles for Radio Eireann and the *Irish Press.*

Behan wrote several stage plays but could not get them performed. Behan's first play to receive a stage production was *The Quare Fellow,* which initially had been turned down by the Abbey. Produced by Alan Simpson in November 1954 at the Pike Theater, it proved an outstanding success, and from that time to the end of his life Behan was a Dublin celebrity. Marriage to Beatrice Salkeld followed the next year. When Joan Littlefield presented *The Quare Fellow* in London in 1956, Behan acquired an international reputation. His next play-writing success was *An Giall,* in Irish, for Gael-Linn the Irish Language Cultural Organization, at the Damer Theatre in 1958. Translated as *The Hostage,* the play was another resounding success when Littlewood produced it in London later that year. Next came Behan's autobiography, *Borstal Boy* (1958), a portrait of the artist as a young prisoner, and the author, who was surely one of the world's greatest conversationalists, was in demand all over Europe and America as a guest on TV talk shows. His two major plays were in constant production around the globe. Behan's later, unfinished play *Richard's Cork Leg,* completed by Alan Simpson and first produced in 1972, has not been successful, but Frank McMahon's brilliant adaptation of *Borstal Boy* for the stage in 1967 created, in effect, another Behan play, one frequently performed and very popular. Behan also wrote several witty and insightful books like *Brendan Behan's Island* (1962) and *Brendan Behan's New York* (1964).

Tragically, the once-poor youth from the Dublin tenements, turned perpetual roaring boy, couldn't handle his success. Alcohol, drunkenness, and diabetes ruined his health and his life. It was a sloppy life but one of meteoric achievement. He died in Dublin on 20 March 1964 at the age of forty-one. His funeral was gigantic. The illegal IRA gave him a soldier's burial. It seemed that all Dublin felt the loss and came out to say farewell to a man they all related to as a beloved personal friend.

In the four years of Behan's high creativity, 1954 through 1958, he reinvigorated the Irish stage with the language of the Dublin working class, with the ironic humor and sardonic wisdom of the disbelieving underprivileged who know that they are born outcasts and that their resistance to authority is ultimately futile—but what the hell! Behan's plays are yet another expression of the ordinary Irish experience. Like O'Casey, he gave voice to the Dublin poor. And in their own way his plays are as political as O'Casey's, depicting common people whose fate is determined by economic forces beyond their control as they are swept up in historical conflicts they barely comprehend.

Plays

The Quare Fellow (1954)

A brilliant and deeply moving protest against capital punishment, *The Quare Fellow* is set in Mountjoy Prison, Dublin, "on the banks of the Royal Canal." Here prisoners and warders are caught up in a culture of oppression and must cope as best they can. The play is based on fact: the execution by hanging of a man who had killed his brother. Behan had known the man in Mountjoy. Because Behan, in his IRA days, could have been executed if shots he had fired at police or explosives he had carried had killed, *The Quare Fellow* may have been his way of coming to terms with his nightmares.

Amazingly, the protagonist, the Quare Fellow, who is continually spoken of and then hanged, never appears, yet he is a very real character indeed. For both the play's characters and the audience, the great suspense is the waiting for the execution. A prisoner, reprieved at the last moment, doesn't know what to do with his life and so he tries to kill himself. Filled with black humor and thematic song, the play is ultimately about human relationships and identity, reduced in the prison to a card on the cell with a name, a religion, and the length of the sentence—in other words, the roll call of life itself.

The Hostage (1958)

The setting of *The Hostage* is a brothel. Once again Behan, like O'Casey, reduces national issues to the level of the individual human beings who are caught up in great issues. But unlike O'Casey, Behan, mocks these issues with his jumble of styles, dance, music hall business, and song.

An IRA operative has been captured and is about to be executed in Northern Ireland; in reprisal, an English soldier has been seized and taken to Dublin as a hostage. The brothel is run by an ex-IRA man but owned by an Englishman who speaks Irish. The soldier falls in love with an Irish servant girl, and the audience hopes love will conquer hatred, but in the end he is executed. His death is more important to Behan than all the issues contested, for Behan's sympathy is always with the individual. Brendan Behan was a big man with a big soul, whose compassion for his fellow humans shines through his drama and his prose.

Additional Reading

Behan, Brendan. *Borstal Boy*. London: Methuen, 1958; New York: Knopf, 1959.
———. *Complete Plays*. New York: Grove, 1978.
Boyle, Ted E. *Brendan Behan*. Boston: Twayne, 1969.
Kearney, Colbert. *The Writings of Brendan Behan*. Dublin: Gill and Macmillan, 1977.
O'Connor, Ulick. *Brendan Behan*. London: Hamish Hamilton, 1970.

15
•••

Brian Friel
(1929–   )

At this writing Brian Friel is the most important living Irish dramatist, a world-famous playwright who has won the championship belt previously worn by Synge, O'Casey, and Beckett. He is at the height of his powers, and a production of a new Friel play is international news. For millions, Friel speaks for Ireland from the stage. Of course, no one today can speak for all of Ireland, but Friel, a Roman Catholic born in Northern Ireland, educated in both the North and the South, and residing in Donegal, not far from the border (sitting on the geographical fence, so to speak), may come closest of all contemporary dramatists. He is an Ulsterman, and even though he now lives in the Republic, his home in Donegal is in the ancient province of Ulster. Furthermore, the consensus is that *Translations* (1980) is the most profound Irish drama of the postmodern epoch.

Friel was born in Omagh, County Tyrone, where his father taught school. In 1939, when Friel was ten, the family moved to the city of Derry, and he received his early education there, first at the Long Tower School, where his father then taught, and then at St. Columb's College. He spent two years at the Catholic Seminary at Maynooth College, County Kildare, receiving the B.A, but without intending ordination. In 1948 he enrolled in St. Joseph's

Teacher Training College in Belfast and then became a schoolmaster in several primary and intermediary schools in Derry from
1950 to 1960. His first play, *The Francophile,* was staged in 1960 at
the Ulster Group Theatre in Belfast; it was later adapted for radio
as *A Doubtful Paradise.* His second and third plays were *The Enemy
Within* (1962), a history play set in the sixth century on St.
Columba's Iona, and *The Blind Mice* (1963), a problem play about
loyalties within and without the Church. Like *The Francophile,*
they are little regarded today.

During his teaching career, writing after work, Friel had
much success as a short story writer for the *New Yorker* and other
magazines, while the BBC produced his radio plays. Friel's short
story collections include *The Saucer of Larks* (1962), *The Gold in the
Sea* (1966), and *Selected Stories* (1979), which was republished as
The Diviner (1982). The skillfully crafted stories are about Ireland's North. They sing the nostalgic song of rural loss, and they
mark the transient but precious moments of life as his characters
seek a meaning beyond survival.

Marriage to Anne Morrison came in 1954 while Friel was still
teaching and struggling to find time to write. The couple have
five children. In 1963, Friel traveled to America to observe, work
with, and learn from the distinguished Irish and international director Tyrone Guthrie as he launched the Tyrone Guthrie Theatre
in Minneapolis. There Friel acquired knowledge of the techniques
of skillfully building plays, and he understudied the ways of the
professional theater.

The great historical, political, and social event of Friel's life
was the resurgence and eruption of "The Troubles," beginning in
1968 with the marches and countermarches, the breakdown of
law and order, the massacre of fourteen Catholic marchers by
British soldiers in Derry in 1972, and the continuing terror, re-
prisals, assassinations, and bombings as the North of Ireland dis-
integrated into a fearful world of police and soldiers facing off

against guerrillas, with a civilian population held hostage to the vast international failure of political imagination. In that maelstrom Friel's art was at least temporarily politicized.

One result of that politicizing was the founding of the Field Day Theatre Company in 1980 by Friel and Stephen Rea in Derry, with the Guildhall as its venue. Its raison d'être was the production of plays that would radicalize audiences and perhaps bring political and social change to Northern Ireland. Field Day, a phenomenon, was an institution that was not restricted entirely to theater but rather, with Derry as its epicenter, had several other cultural facets, including publishing. Seamus Heaney and Seamus Deane were among the Irish luminaries associated with Field Day early on. *Translations* in 1980 was the new northern company's first and greatest production. It should be noted that Friel has not been associated exclusively with one company. His plays have premiered at the Abbey more than elsewhere, but they have also opened at Dublin's Gaiety, Olympia, and Gate; the Helen Hayes Theater and the Longacre Theater in New York; and the Royal Court Theatre and the National Theatre in London.

In 1987 the Republic of Ireland gave Friel the highest recognition it has for an artist: he was appointed to the Irish Senate.

Major plays of Brian Friel include the following ones, in chronological order. *Philadelphia, Here I Come!* (1967), which established Friel's national and international reputations, shows the private and public personae of a young man about to emigrate. *The Loves of Cass McGuire* (1966) treats the returning of an exile: an old, derelict, drunken, embarrassing, unwanted Irish-American woman.

The Lovers (1967) includes two stories: "Winners," with two school dropouts—the girl pregnant—dreaming of their future, although they will die in a boating accident; and "Losers," a comedy in which a middle-aged bachelor tries to prevent the mother of the spinster he is wooing from learning of his intentions.

In *Crystal and Fox* (1968) the head of a rundown traveling

show, Fox Melarkey, destroys his family, his business, his identity, and his and his wife's life in his vain attempt to recapture an ideal and innocent world.

The Mundy Scheme (1969) has Friel satirically wondering if the Republic is actually a nation or a pastoral playground for Europe and America. *The Gentle Island* (1971), symbolically Ireland, is in fact Inishleen, off Donegal's coast, from which most of the islanders are leaving for menial jobs in British cities; the few who remain are caught up in destructive jealousies and feuds. *The Freedom of the City* (1973) is Friel's angry reaction to the killings in 1972. *Volunteers* (1975), like its predecessor, is based on contemporary events, this time in Dublin, where the City Council is destroying the Viking archaeological site to build office buildings, and political prisoners volunteer to work to save what bits of history can be saved while, with the Irish proclivity to self-destruction, their fellow prisoners brand them traitors and threaten their lives.

Living Quarters (1977) like Euripides's *Hippolytus*, depicts, but in an experimental form, the vulnerability and fragility of a family in which the young must extract understanding and values from uncooperative elders or destroy the unit. *Aristocrats* (1979) is an elegy to the end of the Irish Big House as well as an anatomy of a declining Catholic family. *Faith Healer* (1979) is about the artist waiting for the creative miracle, with dire results.

Translations (1980) contains the great theme of the lamented death of the Irish Language. *The Communication Cord* (1982) finds Friel unsentimentalizing Irish rural life, symbolized by a cottage that in the end nature herself destroys, as if in protest against hypocrisy and delusion. *Making History* (1988) deals with the way the future chooses to remember the trials and tribulations of the great Irish soldier Hugh O'Neill and the historically pivotal battle of Kinsale in 1601.

Dancing at Lughnasa (1990) is a ritual drama where the ancient festival of dance and music is reflected in the lives of five unmarried sisters and the unstable men in their lives. *Wonderful Tennessee* (1993), like a medieval text, has each teller telling her or his personal story, which may only approximate truth. In *Molly Sweeney* (1994) Friel, like Synge in *The Well of the Saints*, examines blindness from the point of view of a woman born into it, who is faced with the possibility of partial vision that would change and complicate her life. *Give Me Your Answer, Do!* (1997) is a despairing parable of a novelist's inability to handle the emotional demands on him made by wife, mentally handicapped child, relatives, and friends, when his own creativity has dried up and financial ruin is imminent.

Important also are his translation/adaptation of Chekhov's *Three Sisters* (1981) and his dramatization of Turgenev's *Fathers and Sons* (1987).

For the most part, it is Donegal and Derry that comprise the environment and inspiration for Friel's plays. This is an economically depressed region of high unemployment and much emigration, with an artificial dividing line, the boundary between the Republic and the British province of Northern Ireland, where on the Northern Ireland side Roman Catholics have endured discrimination and political repression at least since 1922, while sectarian strife has simmered and boiled over since 1969.

Friel creates imaginary towns in which he can order events and command fate: Ballybeg (small town) and Ballymore (big town). Ballybeg is a rural town whose old Irish traditions, values, and culture have been continually eroded from the late eighteenth century to the present. It is a town between the cusps of colonialism and postcolonialism.

In a critique of capitalistic and colonial society, Friel's sympathy is with the poor, the dispossessed, the struggling artists, the disenfranchised youths without hope and trapped by the impediments of the past and the crushing weight of institutions. But although Friel's writing is always informed by a sense of historical injustice and imperial oppression and appropriation, there is humor and satire in his work, and the plays are always compassionate. He has tried to remain an observer—to stand above the fray, so to speak—but in the end his compassionate heart, his love for all of Ireland and all the Irish people, and his deeply ingrained loyalty betray and ennoble him.

Plays

Philadelphia, Here I Come! (1967)

Eschewing his usual linear plot, Friel in *Philadelphia, Here I Come!*, splits the character of Gar O'Donnell into two roles, his public and his private self, an attention-getting, theatrical device. Set in his home the night before Gar is to emigrate from Ballybeg to America, the play is centered on relationships that the young man finds difficult to resolve before leaving: his relationship to his beloved town, and, more complicatedly, his relationship to his widowed father, whom he simultaneously mocks, despises, and loves.

The alter ego, a secret sharer, can be heard only by Gar, and thus he is able to say things to—or, rather, at—people that Gar cannot. Nevertheless, they are one person. Gar's chums arrive to bid farewell, and in their reminiscences they portray the paucity and vacuity of small-town Donegal life: the coldness, the spiritual bankruptcy, the repression, the empty streets, the joylessness, the seductions never achieved, and the empty future.

In the course of the play, Gar's mood shifts. He wants to cast off memories of the past, lighten the emotional baggage he will carry abroad, and bring closure to his relationships—father; Madge, the mothering housekeeper; his old schoolmaster; and the girlfriend who rejected him because her father insisted.

Friel implies that Gar can't really communicate with himself, let alone his father. He will go to Philadelphia and live with a mothering, childless aunt, carrying his half-unwanted bag of memories, because it is his destiny to leave and to lose what he loves, and never to love the freedom he has won.

The Aristocrats (1979)

A play reminiscent of Chekhov's *The Cherry Orchard*, and Lennox Robinson's *The Big House*, Friel's *Aristocrats* is set within a Big House, Ballybeg Hall, and on its lawns. The inhabitants are not Anglo-Irish "aristocrats" but Roman Catholics. The house belongs to District Judge Justice O'Donnell, the third generation of high judicial officials. Called Father by his children, he has a startling, commanding voice that is heard throughout the first two acts through the loudspeaker of a baby alarm intercom set near his upstairs bed so he can be monitored downstairs, for he has had strokes, is partially paralyzed, and is demented.

As in *The Cherry Orchard* and *Uncle Vanya*, an old social order is disintegrating, but here the fault is patriarchy, the power of Father, who has debilitated, stifled, and overcontrolled his children—three daughters and a son—until they rebelled by taking up causes repugnant to him, or having a child out of wedlock, or joining a nunnery in Africa, or becoming an alcoholic, or remaining at home as a nervous young woman vaguely content to marry a middle-aged, greengrocer widow with four children, or, in the sad case of the son, Casimir, developing into a self-deluding, fib-telling, timorous effete.

At the end of the second act, Father leaves his bed, collapses, and dies, thus upsetting his youngest daughter's plans to marry. The third act takes place after the funeral. The wedding for which they have all assembled is postponed for three months, and they learn that without the judge's pension the house, which is falling apart, is no longer tenable. As they leave for their various lives and destinations, it is only the husband of the alcoholic daughter who feels a sentimental loss; because his family had long worked for the masters of the Big House, he knew that it was as much his inheritance being lost as it was the loss of Father's children.

Friel is superb in creating the atmosphere of decay, disintegration, and loss as both an epoch and the way of life it supported come to an end. A family has descended the social ladder. There will no longer be Catholic "aristocrats" at Ballybeg House. Still, the world will go on and the children will survive as best they can. It is in the human spirit to do so. Casimir may have the answer: don't expect much from the world and you are safe.

Faith Healer (1979)

Like Akira Kurosawa's *Rashomon*, Friel's *Faith Healer* is narrated from the divergent viewpoints of three characters, each of whom has a spin on shared past events. The play is structured around four monologues: Frank Hardy, the faith healer, offers the first and the last; his wife, Grace, and Teddy, his manager, speak the other two. Frank is a traveling faith healer who is not sure if he has the power. He recollects his successes and failures, traveling through remote areas of England, Wales, and Scotland in a ramshackle caravan, performing each night in small communities, offering the very ill hope of a cure, while waiting for a miracle himself.

Unsure of his effectiveness, he nevertheless is convinced that he responds to real human need. Frank may symbolize Friel the playwright and the doubts that most true artists have about their art. For Frank, like Friel or any other playwright, is a creator of lives, albeit fictions. Frank writes the scenario for his own death at the hands of his people as if he were a mythic old god turned scapegoat, for death, like faith, waits at home for the exile's return. Frank achieves the peace he has sought, but Grace, who has never gotten over the death of their stillborn child and is unable to live without the power of the faith healer that she has resented yet needed, kills herself.

In *Faith Healer* Friel is saying, in a postmodern way, that there are several narratives possible in his story, and that he will not control and force upon the audience one ex cathedra "reading" of the events of the drama. It is as if he, although the writer, denies authority and is merely one of the infinite number of possible commentators or even "crafters" of the story.

Translations (1980)

Considered Friel's masterpiece, and one of the most important Irish political plays ever written, *Translations* treats the ultimate colonization of Ireland in the early nineteenth century, brought about because the British Army Engineering Corps mapped and renamed the countryside in order to facilitate military movement and control. The mapmakers and surveyors themselves may have been well-meaning, but they participated in the devastation of an ancient culture, facilitating its replacement by the colonial culture. English is at war with Irish Gaelic, and it is winning. The struggle is symbolized microcosmically by its effect on a single family in the small town once named Baile Beag but now given the colonial appellation "Ballybeg."

Translations is also about the difficulties and the failures of translating—not only between languages but, more significantly, between cultures. The struggle between languages, the chief conveyors of culture, is always a struggle for power.

The play is set in a hedge school, an outlawed school that taught Greek and Latin through the illegal language, Irish. All such schools were eventually superseded by the National Schools set up in 1831 with instruction in English. The schoolmaster is Hugh, a heavy-drinking pedagogue in his sixties, who stands for the fading authority of the Celtic past. He is the father of two sons: Manus, the older, is a teacher, like his father; Owen, the younger, has returned to Baile Beag from Dublin with the British Army Engineering Corps to serve as a translator, aiding the officers in mapping and renaming the North. Owen has integrated into the greater world of the British Empire, only uneasily, for he still retains feelings for his Irish culture and community.

Owen's friend, the sensitive English lieutenant Yolland, falls in love with Maire, an Irish girl, and she with him. They cannot communicate with language, but love has a powerful language of its own. The audience is led to hope, in vain, that their love and his idealizing of the beauty of the landscape and the warmth of the Irish way of life will serve as the first cable in a great bridge linking the two cultures. *Translations* is a tragedy, and as in history the bridge is never to be completed, for Maire has a jealous Irish suitor, and one day Yolland disappears.

Assuming that his lieutenant has been captured by the Irish, Captain Lancy, the British commanding officer, Captain Lancy, orders that if Yolland is not returned, in reprisal the livestock will be killed, the houses torn down, and the people driven from the area. Manus, sensing a tragedy unfolding, has meanwhile left Baile Beag, but presumably he will be hunted down as a suspect in the disappearance. Presumably also, Yolland has been murdered. Owen, the mediator, the translator, the bestrider of cultures has failed and does not know what now to do with his life.

In the end, communication of language, human understanding, love, and compassion has broken down and failed tragically. The play *Translations*, however, succeeds brilliantly because it clearly proves the efficacy of art in informing, delineating, circumscribing, and clarifying the seemingly insoluble problems of the postcolonial world. It deeply moves the audience to embrace in their hearts the truth that all political disasters in the end are parsed into individual human pain and suffering.

Dancing at Lughnasa (1990)

Brian Friel owes a debt to Tennessee Williams's *The Glass Menagerie* for *Dancing at Lughnasa*, his exquisitely lyrical and sentimental memory play presented through the eyes of a mature narrator seeing himself as a youth and recalling key incidents in early family life. In the case of *Dancing at Lughnasa*, the narrator, Michael Mundy, is remembering a Ballybeg childhood; unlike Tom in *The Glass Menagerie*, he breaks through the fourth wall of the play to provide dialogue for his young persona directly. This is a daring piece of stagecraft, somewhat related to Friel's double character of Gar in *Philadelphia, Here I Come!*

Lughnasa is the ancient Celtic festival honoring Lug, the god of the harvest. The events of this mood play take place during the festival time in a year in the early 1930s but have little to do directly with the festival except in the strikingly effective and moving scene in which the unmarried Mundy sisters—Michael's mother and four aunts—like ancient celebrants, break out in a spontaneous wild and joyous dance to the music from their battery-powered radio. (Their cottage has not been electrified as yet.)

The dance and pagan leitmotivs continues through two additional characters, the adult men within the story. Michael's father, who charms with his skillful ballroom dancing, comes to visit the mother of his child, Christine, the youngest sister. She hopes for marriage, and Michael longs to have a permanent father in his life within the female tribe. But it is a longing not to be fulfilled, for the father, Gerry, is just passing through.

The other male dancer is Father Jack, older brother of the Munday sisters (and thus Michael's uncle), once a priest in Africa but now apparently in forced retirement for having "gone native" and participated in pagan rituals. He treats his surprised and apprehensive sisters to his version of a tribal dance he witnessed. Jack was deeply moved by the "Lughnasa" in his African parish.

The audience learns that the future lives of the sisters are without much happiness or prosperity. The one professionally employed sister, Kate, a teacher in a parish school, loses her job because the community is intolerant of her brother's strange behavior and disturbing paganism. None will marry. No other child will come from the family of the disgraced priest and his sisters.

But it is all in the past, and the mature narrator, unlike Williams's Tom, wants us to share his love of the women of his childhood, his appreciation of their strength and warmth, his pleasure in nostalgia, and his bemused affection for the weak, inadequate men he knew in his youth.

As elsewhere in Friel's dramatic canon, *Dancing at Lughnasa* is slightly marred by excessive narration. Sometimes in Friel the play seems more like a narrated short story than a drama with action as well as characterization. Yet this play in a sense is a dance—a dance of exquisite phrases as well as physical movements.

Dancing at Lughnasa continues to charm, delight, and move audiences all over the world, succeeding wonderfully because of Friel's ability to stoke the memory dramas deep within us all, and project on the stage his engagement with and yearning for the earlier, simpler times in the region of his birth. He invites us to share his passionate love of people—not as vast humanity, but as the individual, ordinary, unsung women, men, and children who comprise the population of his nation. The overriding accomplishment in *Dancing at Lughnasa* is that Friel the playwright there aspired to—and achieved—poetry *of* the theater as well as poetry *in* the theater.

Additional Reading

Andrews, Elmer. *The Art of Brian Friel.* London: Macmillan, 1995; New York: St. Martin's, 1995.

Dantanus, Ulf. *Brian Friel: A Study.* London: Faber and Faber, 1988.

Friel, Brian. *Selected Plays of Brian Friel.* London: Faber and Faber, 1982; Washington D.C.: Catholic University Press of America, 1986.

Maxwell, Desmond E. S. *Brian Friel.* Lewisburg, Pa.: Bucknell Univ. Press, 1973.

O'Brien, George. *Brian Friel.* Boston: Twayne, 1989; Dublin: Gill and Macmillan, 1989.

Pine, Richard. *Brian Friel and Ireland's Drama.* New York and London: Routledge, 1990.

16

Other Contemporary Dramatists

Today Ireland is blessed with an extraordinary number of outstanding playwrights. Professionally, the depth, range, and quality of dramatic activity in Ireland is unmatched in any other
country within Western culture, regardless of size. Other playwrights of Brian Friel's generation include Hugh Leonard (John
Keyes Byrne), John B. (Brenden) Keene, Eugene McCabe, Tom
Mac Intyre, Thomas Kilroy, and Tom (Thomas Bernard) Murphy.
A younger generation is here represented by Frank McGuinness
and other playwrights born in the 1950s, 1960s, and 1970s.

Hugh Leonard (1926–   )

Born in Dalkey, County Dublin, and working first as a civil
servant in Ireland and then as a writer on both shores of the Irish
Sea, Hugh Leonard is a very witty writer with a superb style and
the ability to write drama that is always finely crafted. His best-
known plays are *Stephen D* (1962), an engrossing version of
Joyce's *Portrait of the Artist as a Young Man;* and the autobiograph-
ical *Da* (1973), a perennial favorite, in which Leonard compas-
sionately memorializes his deceased foster father. In *Da*, Leonard
has two actors share a character, as Friel did in *Philadelphia, Here I
Come!* (1964).

Additional Reading

Leonard, Hugh. *Selected Plays of Hugh Leonard.* Gerrards Cross, England: Colin Smyth; and Washington, D.C.: Catholic University of America Press, 1992.

———. *Stephen D.* London: Evans, 1962.

John B. Keene (1928–)

An especially popular contemporary dramatist, and also a novelist, is Kerry-born John B. Keene, whose work sometimes relies on melodrama and sentimentality. Keene is best represented by the frequently revived *The Field* (1965), which is neither melodramatic nor sentimental. In this drama a bullying patriarchal farmer takes his love for a piece of land to such an extreme that he will murder for it, and his close-knit and fearful community is willing to cover up for him. The film version, although considerably changed from the stage version, was a success at art houses in America.

The very enjoyable play about priests and their housekeepers, *Moll* (1971), is a sentimental comedy typical of Keene. Frequently performed by community theaters, it is occasionally revived by professional theaters.

Additional Reading

Keene, John B. *The Field.* Cork: Mercier, 1967.

———. *Moll.* Cork: Mercier: 1971.

Eugene McCabe (1930–)

A graduate of University College, Cork, who was born in Glasgow, Eugene McCabe has devoted his dramaturgic skills and energies primarily to television, but in the 1964 Dublin Theatre

Festival McCabe's *King of the Castle*, a powerful, direct, social drama was a major success. In *King of the Castle*, McCabe, like other writers of his generation, takes on the rapacious values and shameless upward mobility of the nouveaux riches.

Barney Scober, the "king," is a vain, heartless glutton for land. His "castle" is a Big House previously owned by the local gentry. But although they possess the surroundings of the gentry, neither Scober nor his wife, Treasy, will ever have the good taste of the previous inhabitants of the house. Childless, desiring an heir and taunted for his inability to father one, Barney chooses a surrogate father, a farmhand named Lynch, to stud for his wife, and a domestic tragedy ensues.

Another notable success for McCabe was his biographical drama *Swift* (1969), directed at the Abbey by Tyrone Guthrie.

Additional Reading

McCabe, Eugene. *King of the Castle*. Dublin: Gallery Books, 1978.

Tom Mac Intyre (1933–   )

In style, subject, and use of poetic language, Tom Mac Intyre, born in County Cavan, has followed in the footsteps of Synge and Beckett. His reputation was established with *Eye Winker, Tom Tinker* (1972), an episodic play about the failure of violence and the messy complications of politics within a revolutionary group. Mac Intyre's greatest theatrical success was his adaptation for the stage in 1983 (revised 1986) of Patrick Kavanagh's bitter epic poem *The Great Hunger* (1942), directed by Patrick Mason, the Abbey's brilliant contemporary artistic director.

The Bearded Lady (1984) places the rational and the mad at odds. *Rise Up Lovely Sweeney* (1985) shows Mac Intyre's ability to blend poetic language and myth to great advantage. *Dance for Your Daddy* (1987) is Mac Intyre at his creative extremity, combining Freudianism and Surrealism.

Recently, *Sheep's Milk on the Boil (1994),* a contemporary folk play of great poetic vitality and innovative staging, proved that Mac Intyre's talent is undiminished. In the play, set on an island off Ireland's west coast, an earthy couple, Biddy and Matt, celebrate life as they contest with the Inspector of Wrack.

The experimental historical drama *Good Evening Mr. Collins* (1995) finds Mac Intyre breaking new ground yet again as he anatomizes the Irish Puritanism that is anathema to this playwright of sexual joy and love of life.

Other plays by Mac Intyre include *Snow White* (1988), *Kitty O'Shea* (1992), and *Chickadee* (1993). An Abbey production of *The Chirpaun* premiered in November 1997.

Additional Reading

Mac Intrye, Tom. *Sheep's Milk on the Boil.* In *New Plays from the Abbey Theatre: 1993–1995,* edited by Christopher Fitz-Simon and Sanford Sternlicht, 72–110. Syracuse, N.Y.: Syracuse Univ. Press, 1996.

Thomas Kilroy (1934–   )

The son of a policeman, Thomas Kilroy was born in Callan, County Killkenny, and educated at University College, Dublin. Kilroy, a novelist and a university lecturer as well as a playwright, demands much ratiocination from the theater audience. He has been uniquely successful in pursuing parallel careers as a playwright of distinction and an academic critic.

Kilroy's two best-known plays are *The Death and Resurrection of Mr. Roche* (1969), a study of a middle-aged Dublin bachelor, and *Talbot's Box* (1979), the surrealistic and macabre comic story of a Dublin carpenter, a religious mystic who is to be canonized into "the workers' saint" by unprincipled, manipulative people. Both are plays with a view of Dublin working-class and lower middle-class life that shows it to be (at least at the time of the writing) inhabited by people afraid of the system, lacking confidence in society and themselves, sexually repressed, solipsistic and arbitrary in their values, and very solitary.

The O'Neill (1969), a historical drama of the sixteenth century, uses the Irish military hero Hugh O'Neill and his struggle with the English as a symbol for the continuing disunity in Ireland. As the Earl of Tyrone, O'Neill had been brought up in the English court and thus was in himself a site of conflict.

Tea and Sex and Sympathy (1976) is Kilroy's experiment in the Theater of the Absurd. The play depicts a writer's neurotic struggles with his marriage, guilt, sexual impotence, diminishing sense of identity, and—worst of all—his writer's block.

Other recent plays by Kilroy include *Double Cross* (1986), a play about role-playing on the stage and in life, and *Madam MacAdam's Traveling Theatre* (1991), in which theater and transvestitism are seen as ways of both establishing and obfuscating the chimera called identity.

Kilroy's next play, *The Secret Fall of Constance Wilde,* produced by the Abbey for the 1997 Dublin Theatre Festival, has been warmly received by Festival audiences always interested in Oscar Wilde's family.

Additional Reading

Kilroy, Thomas. *The Death and Resurrection of Mr. Roche.* London: Faber and Faber, 1969.

———. *Double Cross.* Dublin: Gallery Press, 1994.

———. *Talbot's Box.* Dublin: Gallery Press, 1979.

Tom Murphy (1935–   )

A native of Tuam in County Galway, Tom Murphy has made his reputation in Britain but has also been associated with both the Abbey Theatre in Dublin and the Druid Theatre in Galway. Murphy is a master of characterization, and although his characters are often drawn from the less than articulate, his dialogue is charged with an energy reminiscent of the shards of language in Harold Pinter and David Mamet. To date he has written twelve full-length plays.

Murphy's shocking, naturalistic tragedy, *A Whistle in the Dark* (1961) remains the high-water mark of a long career as a playwright. Set in the English industrial town of Coventry, the play is the story of Michael Carney, an immigrant to England, a decent hard-working man, who, out of family loyalty, welcomes his Irish father and brothers, "the fighting Carney's," to England. They are a corrupt and brutal band who immediately try to take over the Coventry underworld as they did in their hometown in Ireland. Beneath their violence and aggression are their feelings of social and racial inferiority.

Michael holds back at first but in the end accepts the primitive values of his father and brothers, as the monstrous patriarch of the tribe, Dada, goads him into fighting his youngest brother, who is killed in the brawl. Ultimately, the conflict of the play is a man's interior struggle between conscience and tribe.

The Sanctuary Lamp (1975), set in an abandoned church where from dawn to after midnight two men, former circus workers, relive their past, desecrate the church, mock the clergy, and in the ruined sanctuary, struggle like Beckett's Vladimir and Estragon to endure Limbo. *The Sanctuary Lamp* is a dark Passion Play; like Christopher Fry's *A Sleep of Prisoners* (1952), also set in a ruined church, it is more religiously allegorical than it first appears to be.

The Blue Macushla (1979), a well-crafted, suspenseful gangster thriller, depicts the Irish underworld as a reflection of New York or Chicago, while hinting at an unsuccessful attempt by certain English criminal or government agents to undermine the young nation.

The Gigli Concert (1983) shows the influence of the Hollywood gangster film of the 1930s and 1940s on Murphy. The play is both a version of and homage to the detective *film noir,* with all the conventions of the genre, including the James Cagney–like Irish gunman.

Murphy's more recent plays include *Conversations on a Homecoming* (1985), whose first version was called *The White House* (1972); *Bailegangaire* (Town without Laughter) (1985), a narrative about an old woman trying to finish a story she has been telling her whole life and never given the chance to end it; and *Too Late for Logic* (1989).

Murphy's work is always profound, even as he savages institutions and satirizes film and stage genres. More than many other Irish playwrights, Murphy seems to write almost entirely for the Irish audience, as his playing field is the contemporary Irish psyche, with all its contradictions, and all the confounding, confusing influences that fight to dominate it.

Additional Reading

Elson, John. "Thomas Murphy." In *Contemporary Dramatists,* edited by James Vinson. London: St. James Press; New York: St. Martin's, 1973, 566–69.

Murphy, Tom. *Plays.* 3 vols. London: Methuen, 1992–94.

———. *A Whistle in the Dark.* New York: French, 1971.

Murray, Christopher, ed. Special Issue on Tom Murphy. *Irish University Review* 17, no.1 (spring 1987).

O'Toole, Fintan. *The Politics of Magic: The Work and Times of Tom Murphy.* Dublin: Raven Arts Press, 1987.

Stewart Parker (1941–1988)

Born in East Belfast and educated at Queen's University in Belfast, Stewart Parker died of cancer before he had the opportunity to fulfill great promise as a dramatist. His three historical dramas he called a "triptych," and they are concerned primarily with Northern Ireland. The best is *Pentecost* (1987), which was A Field Day Company triumph. It is the story of a house in Belfast once inhabited by a bigoted Protestant woman, whose ghost regularly appears and continues to spew her hatred, because the house is currently a refuge for a small group of acquaintances, both Protestant and Catholic, avoiding the violence accompanying the 1974 Ulster Workers General Strike, a successful unionist attempt to prevent power sharing in the province.

Parker, a philosophical writer, set for the Irish artist the task of finding or creating "a working model of wholeness" for the people of Ireland. He believed the politicians could never do it.

Additional Reading

Parker, Stewart. *Three Plays for Ireland: Northern Star, Heavenly Bound, Pentecost*. London: Oberon Books: 1994.

Christina Reid (1942–   )

Belfast-born and from a working-class Protestant family, Christina Reid grew up in that city of spiritual and political contestation. Like Stewart Parker's *Pentecost* and Anne Devlin's *Ourselves Alone*, Reid's most successful and most political play, *Tea in a China Cup* (1982), deals with the continuing troubles in the North. The play was runner-up to Mary Halpin's *Semi-Private*, in the one-time *Irish Times* competition for women playwrights, offered in 1982 in conjunction with the Dublin Theatre Festival and entered by 188 women writers. Reid, the author of ten plays, is the best known and most professionally active playwright to come out of that competition.

Tea in a China Cup is a memory play in which members of a Protestant Belfast family relive their lives during the period from World War I into World War II. Through the continuing tea-drinking ritual, the narrator, Beth, born about the time of World War I, sharply illuminates a woman's antiwar and antiviolence perspective on the values and the limitations of the Ulster Loyalist community into the time of the recent Troubles. Men die, often violently, but women wait and watch and live on as if their generations and stories are all one.

Joyriders (1986) uses O'Casey's *The Shadow of a Gunman* as model and prologue for an essay on the dilemma of the North.

Additional Reading

Reid, Christina. *"Joyriders" and "Tea in a China Shop."* London: Methuen, 1987.

Neil Donnelly (1948–   )

Born in Tullamore, County Offaly, Neil Donnelly is a playwright whose work has won success in Ireland, Scotland (at the Edinburgh Festival), England, New York, and Australia. His plays include *Dust* (1972); *The Station Master* (1974); *Upstarts* (1980), his first Abbey play; *The Silver Dollar Boys* (1981); *Flying Home* (1983); *Chalk Farm Blues* (1984); *The Boys of Summer* (1985); *Blindfold* (1986); *Good-bye Carraroe* (1989); and *The Reel McCoy* (1989).

The Duty Master (1995) is set at a boys's public school in England, where Irish-born Patrick O'Rourke is an English master. His wife, Sarah, is a successful artist about to enjoy a one-person exhibit that will move her into the mainstream of the British art world. But the couple are unhappy, and each is having an affair. Patrick is about to offer a divorce to Sarah so he can marry the school secretary.

Patrick is ashamed of his rural Irish heritage. One day his brother Michael, who has stayed on the farm with their parents in Ireland, appears without warning with a girlfriend in tow who is twenty years his junior. The conflicts of the play center on the marriage on the rocks and the Cain/Abel theme, the perennial Irish theme of antagonism between the son who emigrated and the son who remained home on the land. *The Duty Master* is a well-made, pertinent, and engrossing play.

Generally speaking, Donnelly writes about those Irish who for economic reasons are facing exile or are living in exile in Britain or elsewhere. His characters journey through bleak landscapes: Irish ghettos in foreign cities, housing cooperatives, alien schools, and other institutions. They seem to be seeking a lost place in the universe.

Additional Reading

Donnelly, Neil. *The Duty Master.* In *New Plays from the Abbey Theatre: 1993–1995,* edited by Christopher Fitz-Simon and Sanford Sternlicht, 176–244. Syracuse, N.Y.: Syracuse Univ. Press, 1996.
———. *The Station Master.* Dublin: Co-op Books, 1982.
———. *Upstarts.* Dublin: Co-op Books, 1980.

Anne Devlin (1951–   )

An Ulster-born writer, Anne Devlin has had an Irish and a British career; she also currently teaches creative writing at Birmingham University. In her most significant play, *Ourselves Alone* (1985), Devlin interjects three women into nationalist history and dialogue as they struggle to survive the nationalist/unionist violence in the 1970s. The title is a translation of one of the most inflammatory and controversial phrases in modern Irish history: *Sinn Fein,* the name of the political party of uncompromising nationalism that calls for the reunification of Ireland under the Republic.

But in *Ourselves Alone* the phrase is used ironically, because it refers to the women, who alone resist the propaganda and the entire lexicon of violence. The women possess their own bodies, which slogan-chanting men desire but the women will not allow to be politically so inscribed. The mocking, antinationalist, revisionist spirit of Sean O'Casey informs this powerful play.

Did You Hear the One About the Irishman (1981), a *Romeo and Juliet* or *West Side Story*, is about a Protestant girl and a Catholic boy in love, who continue seeing each other after being warned by the terrorist paramilitias to end the relationship. When they refuse they are murdered. Sectarian hate is presented as overriding all human values. *After Easter* (1994), in which the antagonists fighting over a woman's soul are a Communist father and a Catholic mother, is more a feminist drama than a political play.

Additional Reading

Devlin, Anne. *Ourselves Alone*. London: Faber and Faber, 1986.

Marie Jones (1951–)

(Sarah) Marie Jones, a fine actress as well as a fine playwright, was born in East Belfast within sight of the Harland and Wolff Shipyard. She remains based in Belfast. Her forte is comedy that straddles and crosses the Ulster border. Her first play was *The Hamster Wheel* (1990).

A Night in November (1995) is a one-man show in which a Protestant Ulsterman, a clerk who is barely satisfied with his life, has attended the Northern Ireland vs. Republic of Ireland World Cup Soccer qualifying match in Windsor Park Stadium, Belfast, and is disgusted by the anti-Catholic bigotry at a game he loves. "Disguised" as a Catholic, he sneaks off to Dublin and flies to New York with a planeload of fans to support Ireland in the 1994 World Cup. Welcomed and embraced, he learns that there is a common humanity and a patriotism shared by the people of Ireland regardless of their religion.

In *Women on the Verge of HRT* (1996), Anna and Vera, two friends, travel from Belfast to Donegal for the popular singer

Daniel O'Donnell's annual At Home Concert. They are close to Hormone Replacement Therapy (HRT); that is, they are in their forties. Daniel is their lifeline in their otherwise drab and disappointing lives. One is divorced and angry because her former husband has married a younger woman and had another child, and the other is unsatisfied in her marriage. They share a hotel room, flirt with a waiter who looks like O'Donnell, and after a few drinks fantasize about their lives and their desires. The play sparkles with sardonic wit as Anna and Vera whip out one-liners ripping into men and marriage.

Additional Reading

Jones, Marie. *A Night in November.* Dublin: New Island Books, 1995; London: Nick Hern Books, 1996.

Frank McGuinness (1953–   )

Like Friel a son of the North, Frank McGuinness was born in Buncrana, County Donegal. He graduated from University College, Dublin, and began his writing career with poetry. Currently, McGuinness is second only to Friel as an internationally recognized Irish dramatist. His first play was *Factory Girls* (1982), but it was the devastatingly powerful and insightful examination of the roots and degree of Unionist Northern Ireland's intransigence, *Observe the Sons of Ulster Marching Towards the Somme* (1985), that electrified audiences in Ireland, Britain, and the U.S. when it was first produced and in subsequent revivals.

Observe the Sons of Ulster Marching Towards the Somme is the story of eight men of the famous, doomed 36th Ulster Division of the British Army in France in World War I that courageously went over the top and walked to destruction on 1 July 1916 at the military debacle called the Battle of the Somme. The play begins in the present—in the mind of Pyper, the one survivor of the squad of eight, as he is dying of old age in a hospital. Written in four sections, it relives within his mind, and with the aid of ghosts, the dynamics of the relationships that both torment and weld the squad.

The men, including young Pyper, come from different walks of Ulster life, and they pair off according to class, politics, and sexual orientation as they train and prepare themselves for battle. Finally, they go into the holocaust as a unit of committed Orangemen who are, in a perhaps convoluted way, fighting for possession of Ulster by sacrificing themselves in France.

In *Someone Who'll Watch Over Me* (1992), McGuinness achieved another international success. This play is about three men—an Irishman, an American, and an Englishman—seized by Arab kidnappers in Beirut and held hostage, who fight to maintain their sanity and humanity in the face of appalling living conditions and despair. The Broadway production, with the added context of traumatic hostage-takings in recent American history, was especially successful, although the play is as much about resolving Irish-English mutual prejudices and stereotyping as it is about the cruelty of the random, unjust imprisonment of hostages.

Other recent plays of Frank McGuinness include *Innocence* (1996), a life of the artist Caravaggio; *Carthaginians* (1988), about the impact of Bloody Sunday on the people of Derry; *Mary and Lizzie* (1989), Marx and Engels interpreted by Irish women employees in nineteenth-century London; and *The Bread Man* (1990), poetic but the least specific and least successful of McGuinness's plays. The theater world awaits an equal to *Observe the Sons of Ulster Marching Towards the Somme*.

Additional Reading

McGuinness, Frank. *Observe the Sons of Ulster Marching Towards the Somme*. London: Faber and Faber, 1986.

———. *Someone Who'll Watch Over Me*. London: Faber and Faber, 1992.

Michael Harding (1953–   )

Born in County Cavan and now living in Carrick on Shannon, County Leitrim, Michael P. Harding is a fiction writer as well as a dramatist. Five of his plays have been produced at the Abbey: *Strawboys* (1988), *Una Pooka* (1990), *The Misogynist* (1992), *Hubert Murray's Widow* (1996), and *Sour Grapes* (1997).

Hubert Murray's Widow is a shockingly powerful play about the continuing border war between the IRA and the Ulster Constabulary. It combines sexual passion and betrayal with the revenge of a ghost. The surprise ending is riveting.

Sour Grapes expresses Harding's anger and disillusion with the hierarchy and priesthood of the contemporary Roman Catholic Church. In this play a new bishop, who has come from academic life, is accused of sexually abusing one of his former seminarians, a mentally unstable young man. The investigation, handled very badly and primarily at the expense of the victim, provokes deep thought in the audience and raises the question, Who can be trusted with the souls—and, indeed, the bodies—of the young?

Additional Reading

Harding, Michael. *Hubert Murray's Widow*. In *New Plays from the Abbey Theatre: 1993–1995*, edited by Christopher Fitz-Simon and Sanford Sternlicht, 4–69. Syracuse, N.Y.: Syracuse Univ. Press, 1996.

Sebastian Barry (1955–   )

Another drama to achieve international fame, with highly regarded productions in Ireland, Britain, the U.S., Australia, and New Zealand, is Sebastian Barry's heartbreaking memory play, *The Steward of Christendom* (1995). It is the story of Thomas Dunne, an ex-superintendent of the Dublin Metropolitan Police, a haunted man who looks back on his life and work during the early years of the twentieth century when the loyalty of many Irish was divided, indeed fractured.

Barry's work is highly poetical and wide-ranging in subject matter. *Boss Grady's Boys* (1988) is a pastoral play about the vulnerability of the old. *Prayers of Sherkin* (1990) is about Quaker life in Ireland's West during the late nineteenth century. *White Woman Street* (1992) has an American setting, and takes place in the early years of the twentieth century.

Barry is a resourceful wanderer in geography, time, and place, who seems to have returned to the Ireland of today.

Additional Reading

Barry, Sebastian. *The Steward of Christendom*. London: Methuen, 1996.

Niall Williams (1958–)

Born in Dublin, Niall Williams graduated from University College, Dublin, and now lives in West Clare. He is a novelist and nonfiction writer as well as a dramatist. His first play, produced at the Abbey, was *The Murphy Initiative* (1991).

A Little Like Paradise (1995) takes place in and around Jay Feeney's grocery and bar in a village on County Clare's Atlantic coast. The play focuses on the dreams, illusions, and follies of the inhabitants of this atrophying community, seemingly forgotten on the western edge of Europe. The infrastructure of the community has crumbled; most of all, it needs a hospital. The local political leader is ineffective in the Dail although a great talker locally.

A middle-aged love affair is central to the play, and an elderly alcoholic provides comic relief as he "dies" in the bar and is resurrected, becoming a religious celebrity as he recounts his life-after-death experience. The tragic figure in the play is Father McInerney, who tries to keep the community together even as he is dying of cancer and struggling with his weakening faith.

The community, Caherconn, may be doomed to extinction, but it is loved by some, and they will mourn its demise because the hometown remembered as it was or as it could have been seems in recollection "A Little Like Paradise."

Additional Reading

Williams, Neill. *A Little Like Paradise.* In *New Plays from the Abbey Theatre 1993–1995,* edited by Christopher Fitz-Simon and Sanford Sternlicht, 248–315. Syracuse, N.Y.: Syracuse Univ. Press, 1996.

Donal O'Kelly (1958–)

A talented stage and film actor, Dublin-born Donal O'Kelly is a prolific playwright too. Among his stage works are *Mamie Sighs* (1990), his first play at the Abbey; *The Dogs* (1992); and *Trickledown Town* (1994). And then there is the amazing *Catalpa: the Movie* (1995), a "movie treatment version" of an epic rescue of Feinians from the penal colony in Australia in the nineteenth century—a one-man play in which the actor plays all twenty-six parts and the scenery! O'Kelly first performed it and indeed may be the only human capable of so doing.

Asylum! Asylum! (1995), O'Kelly's second Abbey production, is a polemic drama about the Irish government's indifference to asylum seekers. A family civil war takes place between a sister and a brother—the former an activist lawyer, the latter an ambitious immigration officer—as they battle over the life of a Ugandan refugee. O'Kelly is a writer and activist with a finely honed social consciousness. The play is immediately relevant to events concerning the treatment of immigrants in Ireland today.

Additional Reading

O'Kelly, Donal. *Asylum! Asylum!* In *New Plays from the Abbey Theatre: 1993–1995*, edited by Christopher Fitz-Simon and Sanford Sternlicht, 114–172. Syracuse, N.Y.: Syracuse Univ. Press, 1996.

———. *Catalpa: the Movie.* London: Nick Hern Books, 1997.

Vincent Woods (1960–)

Born on a small farm in County Leitrim, Vincent Woods attended University College, Dublin, for a year and then spent much time in Australia and New Zealand. He has had two successes with the Druid Theatre: *At the Black Pig's Dyke* (1992), whose title is a name from mythology applied to the border between Ulster and the rest of Ireland, and *Song of the Yellow Bittern* (1994).

At the Black Pig's Dyke, a technically innovative and poetically driven drama, is a love story. Two lovers, one Catholic and one Protestant, are seeking peace and happiness on the troubled border. Mummers in masks, who are not only entertainers but also murderers (IRA operatives in disguise), fuse the archetypal and the contemporary in a play that is both tragic and humorous.

Set in County Leitrim in the past and in the present, *Song of the Yellow Bittern* is a love story and ghost story simultaneously, based on a famous 1828 paternity suit in which a Protestant woman accused a Catholic priest of having fathered her stillborn child. Woods depicts the tragic repetition of history as the same basic set of events occur in succeeding generations.

Additional Reading

Woods, Vincent. *The Colour of Language.* Dublin: Daedalus, 1994.

Marina Carr (1964–   )

A former University College, Dublin, student Marina Carr has had a remarkable early career. Her plays have had successful runs in Dublin at the Abbey, in London at the Royal Court, and in New Jersey at the McCarter Theatre. Carr's performed dramas include *Low in the Dark* (1989), *The Deer's Surrender* (1990), *This Love Thing* (1991), and *Ullalo* (1991).

The Mai (1994), a major success at the Abbey, tells the story of four generations of women, each of whose lives are tangles of dreams, fantasies, and heart-wrenching disappointments, mitigated only by the love and sense of matriarchy the women share.

Portia Coughlin (1996) was commissioned by Ireland's National Maternity Hospital as part of its Centenary celebration, and Carr based herself in the hospital while writing it. This play, like *The Mai* a woman's drama, portrays a woman in despair who is haunted by the memory of her twin brother, who drowned fifteen years before.

It is Portia's thirtieth birthday. She has been married for thirteen years to a successful businessman and has given birth to three sons, but she is unhappy and depressed, and she has little love for the institutions of marriage and motherhood because of the demands society makes of those institutions. Her escape is through affairs, but they make her even less stable as her life dissolves in fears and fantasies.

At this writing, Carr's next play, *The Bog of Cats*, is scheduled for an Abbey production in 1998.

Additional Reading

Carr, Marina. *The Mai*. Dublin: Gallery Press, 1995.
———. *Portia Coughlin*. London: Faber, 1996.

Martin McDonagh (1971–   )

A discovery of the Druid Theatre, Martin McDonagh's first play indicated that he has a place among the many outstanding young Irish playwrights. *The Beauty Queen of Leenane* (1996) is set in the kitchen/living room of a cottage in the small town in County Galway. The people seem backward in contrast to the Australian TV programs they watch. The contrast is heightened by the fact that relatives return to visit from America while men go back and forth to England to work.

This is Synge country. Maureen, a forty-year-old virgin who is at constant war with her controlling seventy-year-old mother, meets and, because of her mother's selfish interference, loses Pato, her first lover, her playboy of the western world, who wants her to meet him in Boston so that they can continue as lovers and make a life together. The play is a black comedy with horrifying elements and sinister moments of suspense, but it also contains very witty and pointed dialogue. In addition, it is an essay on the continuing strain of violence in rural Irish culture as well as a love story with a sad ending for the heroine, like Pegeen's.

The Beauty Queen of Leenane turned out to be the first of a trilogy set in Leenane, the place where McDonagh's parents came from. The other plays are *A Skull in Connemara* (1997) and *The Lonesome West* (1997).

Also set in the West of Ireland, this time on a remote Aran island, McDonagh's second play, *The Cripple of Inishmaan (1997)*, is about an orphaned crippled boy who is ridiculed and treated roughly by the community. He feels unloved and unwanted although he is cared for by his "aunts," two elderly sisters who are actually unrelated to him. He wants to find out how his parents died, and he longs for the love of a violent young woman ironically named Helen. When a film crew from America comes to the Aran Islands, he goes to them to see if he can get employment as an actor and is invited to Hollywood for a screen test. When he returns to Inishmaan, he finds truth and love.

The play's tone cuts back and forth cleverly from laughter to tears—and is wickedly politically incorrect. McDonagh's eclectic and acerbic vision is devoted to those left behind in the development of modern, prosperous Ireland.

Additional Reading

McDonagh, Martin. *The Beauty Queen of Leenane*. London: Methuen Drama, 1996.

Selected Critical Bibliography

Index

Selected Critical Bibliography

Bell, Sam Hanna. *The Theatre in Ulster*. Dublin: Gill and Macmillan, 1972.

Boyd, Ernest A. *The Contemporary Drama of Ireland*. Dublin: Talbot Press; London: Unwin, 1918.

————. *Ireland's Literary Renaissance*. Rev. ed. Dublin: Maunsel, 1922.

Deane, Seamus. *A Short History of Irish Literature*. London: Hutchinson, 1986.

Ellis-Furmor, Una. *The Irish Dramatic Movement*. Rev. ed. London: Methuen, 1954.

Etherton, Michael. *Contemporary Irish Dramatists*. London: Macmillan, 1989.

Fallis, Richard. *The Irish Renaissance: An Introduction to Anglo-Irish Literature*. Syracuse: Syracuse Univ. Press, 1977.

Fitz-Simon, Christopher. *The Irish Theatre*. London: Thames and Hudson, 1983.

Fitz-Simon, Christopher, and Sanford Sternlicht, eds. *New Plays from the Abbey Theatre: 1993–1995*. Syracuse: Syracuse Univ. Press, 1996.

Forster, R. F. *The Oxford History of Ireland*. New York: Oxford Univ. Press, 1989.

Hogan, Robert Goode. *After the Irish Renaissance: A Critical History of Irish Drama since "The Plough and the Stars."* Minneapolis: Univ. of Minnesota Press, 1967; London: Macmillan, 1968.

————. *Since "Sean O'Casey" and Other Essays on Irish Drama*. Gerrards Cross, England: Colin Smyth, 1983.

Hogan, Robert Goode, and Michael J. O'Neill, eds. *Joseph Holloway's*

Abbey Theatre: A Selection from His Unpublished Journal. Carbondale, Southern Illinois Univ. Press, 1967.

Hunt, Hugh. *The Abbey: Ireland's National Theatre: 1904–1978.* New York: Columbia Univ. Press, 1979.

Maxwell, D. E. S. *A Critical History of Modern Irish Drama.* Cambridge: Cambridge Univ. Press; Washington, D.C.: Catholic University of America Press, 1984.

McHugh, Roger, and Maurice Harmon. *A Short History of Anglo-Irish Literature.* Dublin: Wolfhound Press; Totowa, N.J.: Barnes and Noble, 1982.

Mikhail, E. H. *An Annotated Bibliography of Modern Anglo-Irish Drama.* Troy, N.Y.: Whitson, 1981.

———. *A Research Guide to Modern Irish Dramatists.* Troy, N.Y.: Whitson, 1979.

Murry, Christopher. *Twentieth-Century Irish Drama: Mirror up to Nation.* Manchester, England: Manchester Univ. Press, 1997.

O'Connor, Ulick. *Celtic Dawn: A Portrait of the Irish Literary Renaissance.* London: Hamish Hamilton, 1984.

O hAodha, Michael. *The Abbey—Then and Now.* Dublin: Abbey Theatre, 1969.

Robinson, Lennox. *Ireland's Abbey Theatre: A History 1899–1951.* London: Sidgwick and Jackson, 1951; Port Washington, N.Y.: Kennikat, 1968.

Roche, Anthony. *Contemporary Irish Drama: From Beckett to McGuinness.* Dublin: Gill and Macmillan, 1994.

Waters, Maureen. *The Comic Irishman.* Albany, N.Y.: State University of New York Press, 1984.

Worth, Katherine. *The Irish Drama of Europe from Yeats to Beckett.* Atlantic Highlands, N.J.: Humanities Press, 1978.

Index

Sanford Sternlicht is part-time professor of English at Syracuse University and a poet, critic, and theater director. His works of criticism include *John Webster's Imagery and the Webster Canon* (1972), *John Masefield* (1977), *C. S. Forester* (1981), *Padraic Colum* (1985), *John Galsworthy* (1987), *R. F. Delderfield* (1988), and *Stevie Smith* (1990). He has edited the plays, stories, and poems of Padraic Colum and coedited (with Christopher Fitz-Simon) *New Plays from the Abbey Theatre, 1993–1995* for Syracuse University Press.